THE
RHODE ISLAND
HANDBOOK

MARK
PATINKIN

Illustrated by
DON
BOUSQUET

ISBN 0-924771-49-6

Table of Contents

DEDICATION

This book is for all of you who've been so welcoming, and made me feel so at home, during my years in Rhode Island.

- M. P.

These illustrations are for M.T. Bousquet.

- D. B.

ACKNOWLEDGEMENTS

First, a thanks to the Journal-Bulletin editors who've given me the freedom for book projects—like this one—which have often taxed my time: Jim Wyman, Joel Rawson, Carol Young, Andy Burkhardt and Alan Rosenberg.

I'd also like to thank my publishers, Chuck Durang and Doug Paton. They keep apologizing to me for just being two guys in a garage office with a dream instead of being Random House, but I'll take them over Random House any day.

And now my most important thanks: At the end of the last book I wrote—"The Rhode Island Dictionary"—I asked for more tales of local quirks. I made the same request earlier in some newspaper columns about Rhode Island. Hundreds of kind readers responded. You'll find many of their words, names and stories in these pages. I couldn't have written this without them.

Nor could I have written it without the patience and advice of my wife Heidi. Many have observed that I came here from Chicago 18 years ago—in my mid-twenties—and in time married a local girl. Well, not quite. Not even hardly. The truth is, even though she says "hamburg" instead of "hamburger," she's a fellow transplant. She didn't move to Rhode Island until she was age three.

Which means our three children will always have an edge over us.

They're natives.

INTRODUCTION

I've always envied the way movie-makers get to do sequels. Book writers don't have that chance as often. Usually, when we finish a project, we've said all we have to say about it - maybe even more - and move on.

But last year, I chose a topic for a book that was so vast a writer couldn't possibly get it down in one volume.

Rhode Island.

So here's the sequel.

My first Rhode Island book was about the way we speak. As in, to take a "Food Section" newspaper headline lying next to me as I write this, instead of saying "The Art of the Tart," a Rhode Islander would say, "The Ott of the Tot." No one else speaks that way in America. I called the book, "The Rhode Island Dictionary."

I'm calling this one "The Rhode Island Handbook." In short, Volume I was about our language, Volume II is about our lore. "The Rhode Island Handbook" is about everything else I could think of that makes us unique: our quirks, habits, eccentricities, diet, culture, and especially the way no one here ever uses turning signals.

You may ask: why call it "The Rhode Island *Handbook*"? As opposed to, say, ' *'Encyclopedia.*" Chiefly because 15 years ago someone wrote a book called "The Preppy Handbook," and made $1 million, so I thought using the word 'Handbook' might heighten my chances of being able to afford a cabana (k'banner) at Bonnet Shores (Bonnit Shaws).

I've done one other thing to help with the Bonnet Shores Cabana goal: I'm writing this book with Don Bousquet, the legendary Rhode Island cartoonist. I realized just how legendary after we did the last book together. At one of our book signings, two young women stepped forward in line, positioned themselves in front of him, fell to their knees, bowed their heads and began to chant, "We are not worthy, we are not worthy..." Then, blushing and giggling, they got his signature, scowled at me and walked away.

Another time, when I was signing alone, several women came up excitedly and said, "I can't believe you're really Don Bousquet."

"I'm not," I said. "I'm Mark Patinkin."

For a few seconds, they just stared.

"Oh," one finally said.

"We were hoping for Don Bousquet," said another.

Then they walked away.

Don and I still get to split the royalties, though, so I'm happy to be riding his coattails again.

I would like to continue this introduction, but in "The Rhode Island Dictionary," I spent a week laboring over a beautifully crafted 10-page intro, and later learned the only person who read the whole thing was my mother. Besides, the idea of handbooks is to write short so they can even be read by Generation-X Rhode Islanders whose normal attention span runs between the time "The Plunge" at Rocky Point starts downhill and the time four seconds later when it hits the water.

So let's start.

By the way, I was kidding about that private cabana. After 18 years here, I've become a real Rhode Islander: Give me a bathing suit, a neckchain, and a patch of sand at Skahbruh to watch the big hair go by, and I'll be happy.

THE RHODE ISLAND HANDBOOK

ICE CREAM COMB

RHODE ISLAND: MORE THAN A STATE — A STATE OF BEING.

Those who've lived here long enough know that Rhode Island is not just a place, it's an identity. Most states are simply where you live. Rhode Island is what you are. Here, you don't say, "I'm from Rhode Island." It's, "I'm a Rhode Islander." That's an altogether different perspective. I grew up in Chicago, and I don't think I once heard anyone say, "I'm an Illinoisan."

THE WAY OTHERS SEE US.

Why do we see ourselves as a distinct subspecies? Partly because that's how the rest of the country treats us. Out-of-state, as soon you mention you're from Rhode Island, people say things like, "You're my first one."

That's no exaggeration. Charles Kuralt once wrote a book of essays on the 50 states. He began the one on Rhode Island by doubting we exist. Not only had Kuralt never met anyone from Rhode Island, he writes that he hadn't even met anyone who'd met anyone from Rhode Island.

This reinforces the feeling of being members of an alien race, objects of curiosity. I got a letter from a Providence native named Laurie Jones who was in college in Maryland. "People would actually ask me to say certain words just to amuse their friends," she said. "At parties, the minute I'd say a word ending in 'r' I'd have an instant audience: 'Hey Bob, come over here - you gotta hear this girl talk.' "

But in the end, what makes us a sub-species is not just the way the world treats us, but our own customs. Anthropologists would find our culture as unique as some isolated, lost jungle tribe. We have our own odd food, our own dialect, and even our own mating selection priorities, which favor girls with big hair and guys with 5.0 liter Fire Bird Trans Ams.

A CONVERSATION WITH THE AUTHOR.

Q: Since Rhode Islanders are shaped by the same TV, magazines and catalogs as people everywhere, aren't you stretching it to say we have a unique culture different from the rest of the U.S.?

AUTHOR: Try ordering an eggplant grinda with special source (sauce) in California.

Q: How about aside from food?

AUTHOR: See what looks you'd get in a garden store (goddin staw) in Texas if you asked for a bag of loom.

Q: I'll give you our accents, but our actual words and expressions are the same.

AUTHOR: Not f'nuthin' but, where else in the country, when someone needs to run home to put on new clothes, do they say, "Gotta 'change up' befaw we 'go to cawfee' and check out the 'specials' at the staws. Be back in juss' a seh'in - Ba-bing, ba-bing."

Q: But people in our own region - other New Englanders - understand us.

AUTHOR: Ask any Rhode Islander who's been to college (carl itch) in Boston what their classmates say when they announce, "Layta. Imotta heah, I'm goan home for the weekend to see my motha'in-brothiz, get a haia-cut from my baba downcity, shop at the packie staw and generally, y'know, b'bee, b'bah, b'boo. Oh, jeejet? Maybe we could have a goodbye sangwidge and talk about becoming loyiz - you're still plannin' on appline to Suffix Nights, ahntcha?"

Q: Last question: were any proud natives mad at you for writing a book having fun with Rhode Island's accent?

AUTHOR: Unfortunately, yes. I received an angry letter from Richard Ouellette - now in Minnesota but a native raised in P'tucket. When he got ahold of "The Rhode Island Dictionary," he was incensed at how disrespectfully I portrayed the local dialect. What made him the maddest, he said, was the book-cover cartoon showing a mechanic leaning over a car engine saying, "It's either your cobbarayta or your spock plugs." Mr. Ouellette's miffed response: "The criticism I have involves the pronoun 'your.' Shouldn't you have said, "yaw," or something more Rhode Islandish?"

IS RHODE ISLAND NECESSARY?

A local woman told me of a friend who recently visited from England, observed the local scene for a week or so, and finally said: "Rhode Island's such a funny little state. Is it necessary?"

I love that.

"EXCUSE ME, BUT I COULDN'T HELP BUT NOTICE THAT YOU PUT VINEGAR ON YOUR FRENCH FRIES AND THAT YOU'RE WEARING BROWN SOCKS WITH BLACK SHOES. WHAT PART OF RHODE ISLAND DO YOU COME FROM?"

"Is it necessary?"

The answer is yes. But not for the obvious reasons, such as so New Yorkers have a place to make a right on their way to Cape Cod.

The reason is back in the late 1600s, there was a breed of Americans who couldn't get along anywhere else. So there was no choice but to create a new state where they could put us.

Many have chronicled our historic orneriness over the years. H.P. Lovecraft, the horror writer who lived here, once described Rhode Island as, "That universal haven of the odd, the free and the dissenting."

But the following excerpt from a history written in 1889 proves it's no exaggeration to say we ended up the retreat for the most cantankerous of colonial types: "As for Rhode Island, it was regarded with strong dislike by the other colonies. It became the refuge of all the fanatical and turbulent people who could not submit to the strict and orderly governments of Connecticut and Massachusetts."

Rumor is many of us are still that way.

So yes, Rhode Island is necessary.

A ONE PARAGRAPH BIOGRAPHY OF ROGER WILLIAMS.

People have written whole books about the guy who founded Rhode Island - Roger (Radjah) Williams - but I'll sum him up in two sentences: "Strange guy leaves England because he can't get along and goes to Massachusetts where he can't get along either, so instead of at last learning to get along, he says, 'Forget you people,' and starts his own personal state. Other ornery Americans read about it in the paper, look up from their apple pandowdy and say, 'Look Hortense, a state just for us.' And they move here." (Sorry, that was three sentences.)

A KEY REASON RHODE ISLANDERS LOVE RHODE ISLAND.

I still remember one of the first moments that made me feel truly at home in Rhode Island. I'd only been here a few months and, as an outsider, was feeling disconnected.

Then, one afternoon, while walking down Thayer in Providence, I saw a thin, dark-haired young woman. She seemed vaguely familiar. Suddenly, she stopped and pointed at me.

"Chicken with apricot glaze," she said.

I stopped.

"Pardon?"

"Chicken with apricot glaze," she repeated. "And don't tell me. Chocolate lady finger mousse cake."

Finally, I placed her. A waitress at a nearby restaurant. I'd been there only twice, and both times ordered the two things she'd just accused me of.

I don't think I'd have been stopped on a sidewalk like that in Manhattan, or Boston.

But that's Rhode Island: a whole state that feels like a small town.

WHY IT'S BETTER TO LIVE IN A SMALL PLACE LIKE RHODE ISLAND THAN A BIG PLACE LIKE NEW YORK

• If you go to a Pawsox game at McCoy Stadium with a party larger than four, you can get announced.

• You get to refer to our chief executives not as Governor Garrahy, Governor DiPrete and Governor Sundlun, but Joe, Ed and Bruce.

• You get to call the mayors of major cities by their nicknames. There has not been a recorded case of anyone in Rhode Island referring to Mayor Cianci as "Mayor Cianci" in years. It's simply "Buddy."

• If invited, any of the above will not only show up as speaker at your organization's annual banquet, but as guest at your family's Christening, Bar Mitzvah or wedding. And even if not invited, they'll show up at your funeral.

• A traffic jam on the interstate is when cars slow to 45.

• There has never been a single mugging on a Rhode Island subway.

"HOW MUCH WOULD YOU EXPECT TO PAY FOR RHODE ISLAND AND PROVIDENCE PLANTATIONS...? WAIT, DON'T ANSWER, BECAUSE WE'LL ALSO INCLUDE THIS MIRACLE MAIZE PROCESSOR AND THREE PIECE SET OF DELUXE STEAK KNIVES... NOW HOW MUCH WOULD YOU PAY?"

THE DOWNSIDE OF LIVING IN A SMALL PLACE LIKE RHODE ISLAND.

• You cannot have an affair. No matter how isolated and secretive the restaurant you pick, you will run into your brother-in-law (brothin-lawr.)

• At Green Airport, you have to walk onto the tarmac and whistle for the airplanes.

MY FAVORITE TRUE RHODE ISLAND STORY.

Charlie Bakst, political editor of the Providence Journal, has lived a long time in Barrinton. A while back, he ran into a neighbor he hadn't seen in years. During that period, the neighbor had grown from a little kid into a young man. Charlie asked what was new.

The young Barrington man said he'd gotten married.

"Anyone from around here?" Charlie asked.

"Nah," said the young man. And then added: "Riverside."

A few miles away.

Only in Rhode Island.

WHAT MAKES A REAL RHODE ISLANDER

It takes time.

The instant you move to California, for example, you're a Californian, since no one is really from there anyway.

Rhode Island is different.

As I write these words, I have a six-month old son, born in Women and Infants' Hospital — which makes him a Rhode Islander. Me? I've been here 18 years, that's 36 times longer than my son, but I remain a transplant.

The word "transplant" itself is further evidence. You don't hear that word in many states; in Rhode Island - you hear it regularly.

Everyone who has been in California a few years is part of one big category: Californians. In Rhode Island, there are two categories: native and transplant.

TRANSPLANTS

There's a story about the couple who summered in Rhode Island for years, finally realized their dream of moving here, and soon after, while sitting on the porch of their just-bought house, were visited by an old neighbor - local Yankee stock - who asked how they liked it.

They answered that they were thrilled to finally be real Rhode Islanders. The neighbor, a native, studied on this a while, then said, "My cat had her kittens in the oven, but that don't make them biscuits."

So we who weren't born here are transplants.

But I'm even proud to have earned that term - it's a step up from "visitor" which is what you're considered for your first five or so years here. That's understandable in a place where most go back a few generations and many trace their roots to the moment Roger Williams rowed up to the head of Narragansett Bay and said to the waiting Indians, "What Cheer, Netop?" Which was native for, "How come all the canoes down here turn left from the right-hand lane?"

THE TRANSITION TO REAL RHODE ISLAND

All transplants initially find the local culture exotic, but something soon changes that: we begin, without realizing it, to take on the traits of real Rhode Islanders.

When I first arrived, every day around noon, colleagues at work would stop by my desk and cuss at me. At least that's what I thought at the time because they said something that sounded like a curse-word.

"Jeejet."

I would stare back blankly. It was only later that I realized "jeejet" was Rhode Island for "Did you eat yet?"

For a while, I thought that an odd expression, but the point here is that after a few years, each day at noon, I suddenly found myself approaching colleagues and saying "Jeejet," too.

I was also at first appalled by Rhode Island drivers. But soon, like a true local, I began squealing left in front of oncoming traffic the instant the light turned green.

I couldn't understand this behavior at first but then it dawned on me: after a few months of breathing Ocean State air, you start acting like a Rhode Islander.

WHY RHODE ISLAND IS LIKE THE INVASION OF THE BODY SNATCHERS.

For those not familiar with it, "Invasion of the Body Snatchers" is a movie about alien beings who take over the world with a subtle trick: In essence (more or less), anyone who comes into contact with them gets transformed into one of them. Those of us who are transplants understand this is how Rhode Island works.

Most move here feeling it will be a brief stop, maybe a year or two. Then we wake up 15 years later still here - and it's not even like we get stuck, we end up liking it. Loving it. And even asking where the bubbla is.

My ultimate example of Rhode Island's body-snatching powers is a doctor at the state's General Hospital. I once interviewed him for a story, then asked his background. He said he'd been in Rhode Island 35 years...by mistake.

He explained that back in the 1950s, he was trying to drive to Long Island, got confused and ended up in Rhode Island instead. But once here, the state got ahold of him and he never left. I'm not making this up; you can ask him. His name is Dr. Baruch Motola.

I met someone on Block Island who ended up a Rhode Islander similarly. He was sailing with his family and forced to tie up there by an approaching storm. But once it passed, it was too late. His body had been snatched by Rhode Island. He decided to stay, quit his job in the New York area and opened a dockage service.

ADMIRING THE VIEW FROM THE
OBSERVATION DECK AT T. F. GREEN AIRPORT

MY ULTIMATE RHODE ISLAND TRAIT: GIVING DIRECTIONS NOT BY STREET NAMES, BUT LANDMARKS.

Growing up in Chicago, I gave directions the normal way: "You go north on Michigan, left on Randolph and right on State." So after first moving to Rhode Island, I was thrown by the way no one here ever mentioned a street when giving directions.

Instead, it was: "You go straight until you hit the NHD hardwear (hodweah) store, take a right, then a left at the playground with that big thing in the middle..."

But after a few years, I found myself doing the same thing. One day, my brother was in town, and I had to give him directions from my East Side home to the Biltmore. Instead of saying, "You go west on Angell, through Kennedy Plaza and take a left on Dorrance," I said this:

"All right, you go downhill past the Brown University Bookstore, stop for the students who always cross on the red, then keep going downhill past that lawyer's office on your right with the Mickey Mouse sign in the second floor window."

And then I actually said: "After that, you go by the railroad overpass they tore down four years ago."

That's my truly ultimate Rhode Island trait: I not only give directions by landmarks, but by landmarks that are no longer there. We all do it.

As in: "You take a right where they closed the Dairy Mart and head to where the movie theater was before they demolished it. Then you take a left after that big elm tree they chopped down to make room for the condos they never built. After that, you go past the street where "The Lying In" used to be..."

THE WAY WE RELENTLESSLY CHANGE NAMES OF THINGS BUT STILL CALL THEM WHAT THEY WERE CALLED IN THE FIRST PLACE.

I think I spent my first 10 years in Rhode Island searching in vain for the Red Bridge to East Providence. I kept running into a bridge, but figured it was the wrong one since it was steel and concrete, not red. Only later did I find out they tore down the Red Bridge decades ago, and replaced it way back in 1969 with something dubbed The Henderson Bridge, after George Henderson who served as the state's chief highway engineer.

But it doesn't matter, poor George will never achieve the immortality he deserves since people will forever refer to it as The Red Bridge. Actually - although it's over 25 years old and not red anymore - many call it The New Red Bridge, rebelling against a government so tyrannical as to actually rename (horrors) a public edifice.

We refuse to call just about everything by their new names. I did it myself just ten minutes ago when I needed to check a fact in this book and called Directory Assistance asking for the number to the General Hospital. The operator told me she couldn't find it. I got annoyed and told her to look harder. Then I remembered. They'd renamed it the "Eleanor Slater Hospital." But it could be well into the next century before people here start calling it that. My guess is that 90 percent of people reading this still thought it was officially the "General Hospital."

There are examples wherever you look.

I'm told that many in Rhode Island still refer to Green Airport as "Hillsgrove."

And URI as "State."

Some may chuckle at this trait as quaint - but when was the last time you directed someone to Newport by way of the Verrazano and Pell bridges?

Of course, I don't want to presume this habit is universal, so if you disagree with my local "old names" theory, I'd be glad to meet you at that coffee shop next to the Industrial National Bank downtown and discuss it. You know the building I'm talking about - it's not far from where The Outlet once was.

Oh, correction. I got a note from an old-time native who said that calling it the Industrial National Bank is even wrong. The proper term, said Frank Vivier of Pawtucket, is the "Industrial Trust Building." Which is to say some natives call things by the names they had not one lifetime ago - but two lifetimes.

Another reader's observation came from Mrs. B.C. Reynolds, a native now living near Tacoma, Wash., who told me that a Providence restaurant called "Murphy's Keyhole Lunch," used to advertise its location as - word for word here - "Across the street from where Fay's Theater used to be."

And most Rhode Island homeowners will concede that even though they've lived in their house for say, 25 years, many neighbors will still call it not "the Smith house," after the current occupants, but "the Jones house" after the people who owned it 25 years before

NOT ONLY DO WE GIVE DIRECTIONS BY LANDMARKS, WE DESCRIBE THE LOCATION OF OUR HOME TOWNS THE SAME WAY

I got a letter from Rich Pichette who kindly told me he never misses my column and reads it every day after the sports, comics, world news, local news, obits, classified, food section, amusements and horoscope. And I thank you for your support, Rich.

Anyway, beneath his signature, he listed his street address, then followed it with, "Glendale, R.I." Anticipating my reaction, he added a PS: "I know, where is Glendale?"

Did he then tell me where it is the normal way, by saying, "It's in Burrillville"? No such luck. Rich is a Rhode Islander. So he described where Glendale is the Rhode Island way:

"It's a half mile south of Wright's Farm," he said.

And if you have to ask what Wright's Farm is, you've got a ways to go before you can claim you're a true local.

(Hint: They don't raise corn or cows there; they serve chicken.)

YOU KNOW YOU'RE A REAL RHODE ISLANDER WHEN...

• You look upon turning signals as optional equipment.

• You don't take your clothes to the cleaners anymore; it's the cleansers (cleansas).

• You've begun to envy cars with low number (lo-numba) plates.

• You describe people you don't like as NG.

• Your drink of preference in warm weather is Del's lemonade slush.

• If five flakes of snow start falling at 9 a.m., you leave work at 10 a.m.

• And head to the supermarket.

• Where you stock up on bread and milk.

THIS WHOLE THING ABOUT RHODE ISLANDERS NOT WANTING TO TRAVEL DISTANCES ISN'T REALLY TRUE, IS IT?

It is. I spoke once with a man who worked in placement for a Rhode Island vocational school. His work was to match students with jobs. Over the years, he helped thousands, but throughout, ran into a basic problem.

If a job was more than 15 minutes from a students' home, the majority, he said to me, refused to take it. Emphasis on the word 'majority'.

They told him it was too far to drive.

MILES? OR MINUTES?

And think about the way we estimate distances when directing someone. In other states, it's always, "Oh, I'd say it's around ten miles from here."

In Rhode Island, it's never miles.

It's always - "About ten minutes."

How many minutes: that's how we view the world.

EXAMPLES OF RHODE ISLAND "DISTANCE-PHOBIA"

• While in New Jersey, Martha Crossley and her husband both commuted an hour to work and no one they knew thought anything of it. Then they both took jobs in Pawtucket - but chose to live in Woonsocket. "We were queried for months by everyone we encountered as to why we would willingly choose to inflict ourselves with a 25 minute commute," she wrote me. "We were treated with both pity and some reservation since it was assumed we had something we wished to hide from our employer that necessitated putting 19 miles between ourselves and our jobs."

• Donna Hilbert of Westerly remembers her family heading for Rocky Point when she was a teenager. When her mother packed "lunch," it would always be enough food for several days. "In case," she explained, "God forbid, the car breaks down, that way we wouldn't

starve." Then, to prove it wasn't just her family's habit, but a Rhode Island habit, she added: "All of our neighbors were filling their trunks with the same things."

• Janet Phillips, formerly of Burrillville, told me of a local heating oil salesman making a delivery to a Swamp Yankee woman deep in the north Rhode Island woods - a Swamp Yankee being a crusty, rural Rhode Islander. The Swamp Yankee woman began complaining about having to go into the city that day, and how much she dreaded the downtown congestion and noise. As Janet relates it, the Burrillville delivery man said, "I know what you mean, I really hate that part where 95 runs into 195. And Providence parking is a hassle." The woman stared at him, then said, "Providence? I'm talking about Pascoag."

• And you know all those jokes about Rhode Islanders who drive 45 minutes across state, and then get a motel so they don't have to drive back the same day? Exaggeration? Tell that to Donna Burns who wrote me of something that happened only a few years ago. "An aunt and uncle from Providence were only able to get 9 p.m. tickets for a show at Matunuck's Theater-By-The-Sea," she said. "They didn't want to drive, 'all the way back' to Providence when the show ended because it was 'too late at night,' (So they said); so they stayed at the Willows Motel and returned home the next morning!!!"

• Dorothy Buckbee of Pawtucket came here from New York in 1950 and soon got a taste of Rhode Island's concept of distance when a Pawtucket neighbor said her husband had a "traveling job."

How far did he have to travel?

He worked in Cranston.

RHODE ISLAND WANNABEES.

There's one subspecies of Rhode Islanders who have never lived here but are kind of official locals anyway: border Rhode Islanders (Bawda Roe Dyelindas).

These are people who live within ten miles or so of the state line, read our newspapers, watch our TV and generally spend their lives thinking they're Rhode Islanders even though they're not.

Jeanne Mccarthy who lives in the direction of Taunton is one.

"It is interesting how we in southeastern Mass. have such an affinity for 'Roe Dyelin', " she wrote to me. "We are not only close in distance, but also in heart and share so many similarities it seems we should be part of Rhode Island." She went on to ask: "Is that a quirk of sorts?"

She then brought up one of the ultimate examples of Rhode Island wannabeeism: Alpert's Furniture of Seekonk.

That's Seekonk, Massachusetts.

But Alpert's has been known to advertise that they sell "more furniture than any store in Rhode Island." Now that's grammatically correct, since they aren't *in* Rhode Island. But they want us to *think* they are, so they hope we'll hear that "they sell more than any *other* store in Rhode Island."

Or maybe they just wannabee Rhode Islanders *soo-o* badly...

I LIKE RHODE ISLAND BECAUSE

• Aside from Michelangelo's David, the Independent Man is the coolest statue in the world.

• You can live on a farm 20 minutes outside the capital.

• Or in a house two minutes from downtown with a suburban-sized yard.

• A guy who signed the Declaration of Independence is buried in Newport.

• We have our own personal shellfish, one that no one else even knows how to pronounce.

• We elected the first female attorney general in the nation's history.

• If you leave Providence at 11:45 to catch a noon plane, you'll make it.

• The longest professional baseball game ever (33 innings over 8 hours and 17 minutes) was played in Pawtucket.

• Sideburns were named after a Rhode Island Civil War general - Burnside - who wore them.

- We have not just a First Baptist church but THE First Baptist Church.

- And the country's oldest synagogue.

- And the tolerance on which we were founded is still in the state's soul.

UNANSWERABLE RHODE ISLAND QUESTIONS

1. Why do so many Rhode Islanders aspire to be in the local mob when the reward is being given a nickname - always printed every time you're mentioned in newspaper crime stories - like 'The Moron'?

2. Why will people in the Providence metro area never drive to Westerly or Woonsocket because it's too far, but until Foxwoods was built, would take buses to Atlantic City five times a year?

3. Why, even when the local unemployment rate approaches 10 percent, does every corner store and fast food place in town have windows plastered with "Help Wanted" signs?

4. Why do Rhode Islanders pronounce "lore" as "law" and "law" as "lore"?

5. Why is "parka" pronounce "pokker" and "pocket" pronounced "parkit"?

6. Why does everyone in the state instantly know who "Junior" (Joonya) is, but half can't name their congressman?

ONE ANSWERABLE RHODE ISLAND DILEMMA

Q: Why do almost all of Rhode Island's richest blue blood East Side families with their huge houses and proud Yankee heritage have such old, frayed, unmodern decor inside?

A: Because the richest of them all still have the old Yankee ethic of making money but never spending it. Meanwhile, these are the very souls who always show their houses at the Preservation Society's annual walking tour of homes in Providence. Other Yankees go on this tour, and that's where they all get their decorating ideas.

YOU KNOW YOU'RE NO LONGER IN RHODE ISLAND WHEN:

• You've driven five miles in a populous area and haven't passed a "Dunkin Donuts."

• And your first reaction is: "What do the police eat around here?"

• You ask the waitress for a grinder and she gives you directions to Home Depot.

• The car in front of you is using turning signals.

• People have random numbers on their license plates instead of names or initials.

• You ask the 7-11 clerk for coffee milk and she points to a nearby set of hot coffee pots - self-serivce - while apologizing that they only have cream.

• No one wishes you Happy St. Joseph's Day.

• Or happy Victory Day.

• And people look at you funny when you speak of Columbus Day as a major holiday.

• Motorists stop for pedestrians.

• Your new friends start asking you to repeat words like "Car, pizza, potato, idea, barber, chowder, and 'the both of you' " for their amusement.

• In September, no teachers are on strike.

• You ask the waitress for vinegar on your French fries and she calls restaurant security.

• Then you order snail salad with your grinder, with little necks for an appetizer, and she faints.

• And a final observation sent my way from Jack Kavanagh, former Rhode Islander and news anchor who moved to Sacramento, Ca. but only, he adds, in body, not spirit. "You have the mob," he said, "we have gangs. If I had to choose between the two, I'd go with the mob."

"BELIEVE IT OR NOT, SOME GUY FROM
RHODE ISLAND ORDERED A GRINDER
AND A CABINET!"

RHODE ISLAND MIXED MARRIAGES BOUND TO CREATE GREAT ADJUSTMENT DIFFICULTIES.

1. Any marriage between a native and an out-of-stater. (Excuse me, Reverend, I don't mean to interrupt from here in the front pew, but what does my future daughter-in-law mean by, "Til Death Do Us Pot?"

2. Where the groom's ancestors are from the south of Italy (Itlee) and the bride's from the north.

WORDS I WISHED I'D HAVE PUT IN "THE RHODE ISLAND DICTIONARY."

It would take another whole book to include all I missed. Virtually any word with the letter "r" has a Rhode Island version. Let me restate that. "Veuht-chili any weuhd with the letta ah has a Roe Dyelin veuhsion." But let me add a few.

Meatbowls - (Enhances Pahster.)

Furrinahs - (Anyone who lives outside ah bordas.)

Ammana - (I am going to.) (Derived from "I'm gonna.)

Smittle - (Naybahood where the Genrasemblee is.)

Undaweahs - ("I always fold my undaweahs afta takin them outta the dry-a.")

Croler - (Model of Toyoter.)

Barkin - (What you get at Skvatch and Dent sales.)

Motta - (Someone who likes to suffa.) (PS: That's "martyr" by the way, not "mother." Though some say the two words are synonymous.)

Hah-rah - (Horror.)

Torque - (Talk.)

Yerp - (Continent west of Ay-zher)

Cahdeez - (Sells sofer conveuhtibles.)

Coupla t' tree - ("Two or three".)

Haitch - (H.)

Sta - ("Good morning, Sta. I'm sahree but I di'int finish my homeweahk. And all my pleadd skeuhts ah at th'cleansas.")

And there's one more I came across following the "Dear" at the top of a letter I received written in Roe Dyelindese:

Mob Dinkin. (My name.)

Oh, and a last one from Stephen Gross who sent me a letter saying he saw the following ad put out by the Salvation Army: "Chester Draws, $55." Gross added: "Must be a famous New England furniture maker.)

THE CHEER ONLY RHODE ISLAND CHEERLEADERS CAN CHEER AND ONLY RHODE ISLAND FANS UNDERSTAND.

"Hiddum again, hodda, hodda."

THE DIALECT TERM I SEARCHED FOR IN VAIN LAST BOOK AND FINALLY FOUND THIS TIME.

A basic Rhode Island speech trait is to leave out the middle consonant of a word like "didn't," and replace it with a sharp break. As in "Dih'int." Or "Bah'ul" - like Bah'ul of 'Gansett Beah. In "The Rhode Island Dictionary," lacking creativity, I simply called it "a break."

But afterward, native Carla (Cahlla) White finally gave me the term for this:

"The Rhode Island Glottal Stop."

One of her favorite Glottal Stop cities, she explained, is New Brih'in. No out-of-stater could ever figure how to pronounce that by reading it on paper; you have to have lived here to know the Glottal Stop.

By the way, Carla has lived in San Francisco for many years now, which raises the question of how a woman long gone from Warwick could retain such a grasp of local quirks. She herself explained it:

"You can take the girl out of 02888, but you can't take the 02888 out of the girl."

SINCE WRITING "THE RHODE ISLAND DICTIONARY," HAS ANYONE ASKED ME WHAT MY FAVORITE LOCAL WORDS ARE?

Yes. My very favorite: D'boatayuz - (Both of you.)

Second favorite: P.S.D.S. (Pierced ears.)

Third: Bah'day'dah - (What Dan Quayle couldn't spell).

DEAH IAN LANDIZ (DEAR ANN LANDERS)

Dear RI Problem Solver: "I just went out on a comp case with a bad back I severely injured on the job. What's the appropriate activity to do over the next year or two while I recover?"

Answer: Power Lifting at Gold's Gym.

TOP REASON FOR COMING BACK TO RHODE ISLAND AFTER BEING OUT-OF-STATE.

• So you don't have to listen to people with peculiar accents anymore.

THAT'S A JOKE, RIGHT - ABOUT RHODE ISLANDERS THINKING THEY HAVE NO ACCENTS?

Tell that to native Jeanne McCarthey. "One memory I have as a child," she wrote me, "was watching national TV news with my cousins. I thought it was so funny the way the broadcasters talked - little did we know as innocent children that WE were the ones who talk 'funny' to the rest of the U.S."

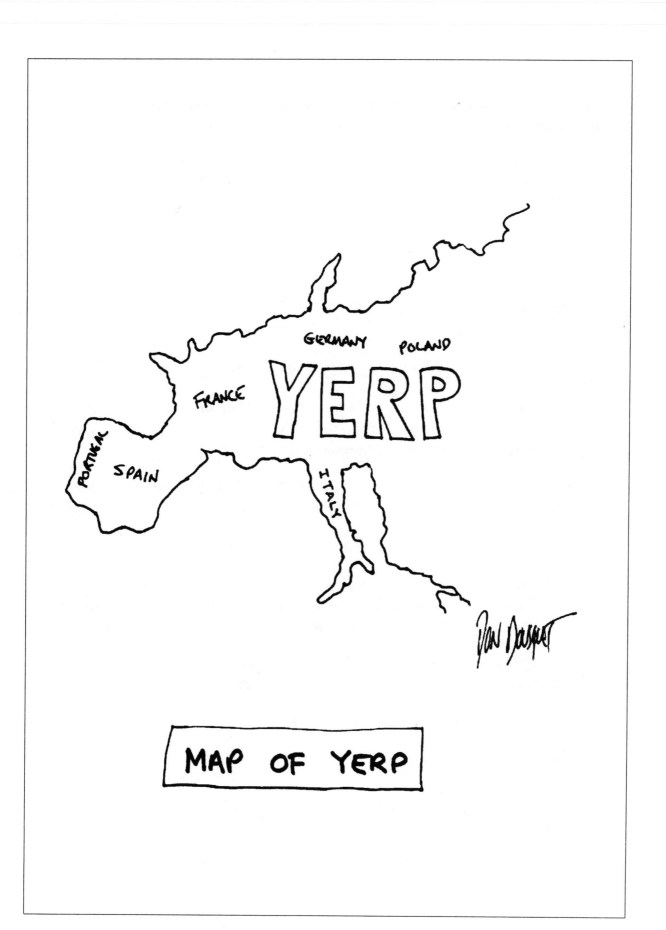

MAP OF YERP

And I've spoken with many Rhode Islanders who for a while in childhood thought certain words were spelled like they're pronounced:

Cards as Cods.

Chimney as Chimley.

Law as lawr.

Polka as poker...

Drawer came out as Draw

THE RHODE ISLAND BOND

You know how two strangers, upon being introduced, feel an instant link when they discover they grew up in the same neighborhood? Rhode Island is one of few places where you feel that way about anyone from the whole state.

When you're out-of-state, or calling out-of-state, and suddenly find yourself speaking to someone from Warwick, or Westerly, or Burrillville - it's like you've discovered a long lost family member. Immediately, you let your guard down: you're with a compatriot who knows about quahog chowder, vanity plates and drivers who fake left and turn right.

Recently, I was speaking by long-distance with a woman named Ann Crumb, a Vermont college administrator. It was all very formal until, halfway through the call, she told me she was from Rhode Island. Right away, we were old friends.

Well, almost. I say "almost" because in this case, she had zero local accent. I mean 'zero'. She spoke in perfect 'network anchor' English. So I decided to test her.

"Ann," I said, "say 'bubbler' in Rhode Islandese."

She didn't skip a beat.

"Bubbla."

I'd found a comrade.

HOW AMERICA SEES US: THE RODNEY DANGERFIELD OF STATES

It's true - we get no respect. I remember seeing a political cartoon that portrayed how Americans view each state. Florida, for example, was marked with the words, "Old People." There was a Midwest state marked "Cows" and one marked "Corn." Nevada, I think, was marked "Gambling." Vermont was marked "Itty," and New Hampshire "Bitty." Finally, there was Rhode Island, which, as is often the case, was so tiny on the map there was barely room for even an outline. But even more telling, it was the only state that didn't even merit a humorous word. The cartoonist drew such a blank on us that all he could think to do was label us with a question mark.

Like I say, no respect.

YOU KNOW YOU'RE A REAL RHODE ISLANDER WHEN...

• If a restaurant's more than five minutes away, it's out of the question.

• In fact, if you call your neighborhood Chinese place and find they're closed, no matter how much you have your heart set on a plate of Hun Yung Gai Ding, the prospect of driving ten minutes to a more distant Chinese restaurant is so daunting you open a can of tuna fish instead.

• You - or at least I - realize that if I took away three restaurants, one Dairy Mart, one beach and one movie theater, there wouldn't be much left of my Rhode Island.

• Someone tells you they don't like something - for example, "Call-Waiting" - and your form of agreeing is to respond, "So don't I."

• You order an iced coffee in December.

• You know two-thirds of the state, once-removed.

• At work in Warwick, when you see a colleague from a place as far away as Scituate, or even Western Cranston, you ask, "How's the weather up there?"

• Instead of going to the liquor store, you make a packie run.

• Your son brings home a girlfriend with big hair from Cranston East named "Chevul."

THE RODNEY DANGERFIELD OF STATES, CONTINUED...

It's as if national humorists feel that when they need a laugh, all they have to do is mention the words, "Rhode Island." They can be confident everyone in America will snicker and say, "Right - that tiny, minuscule little place that could fit in my living room and has no business being a state in the first place."

Remember the movie, "Arthur" with Dudley Moore? One of the biggest laugh lines is when he stumbles into the Plaza Hotel with a prostitute in tow. As he sits down to dinner, some friends come to his table. Arthur doesn't want them to know who she is, so he tells them she's a princess. From a country in Europe.

Which country?

Oh, just a small one, says Arthur, babbling on to cover his fib. Very small. Tiny, really.

How tiny?

"Rhode Island could kick its fanny."

Then there was a character named Lola in "Damn Yankees" who sold her soul to the devil to avoid what was presented as about the most horrible imaginable plight on earth. Part of the plight is that she was ugly.

But it was even worse than that.

Her words:

"I was the ugliest woman in Providence, Rhode Island."

SO WHAT'S THE MAIN THING RHODE ISLAND IS KNOWN FOR NATIONALLY?

Some would say Brown University. In fact our politicians often cite that at presidential nominating conventions when the head of the Rhode Island delegation stands to announce how many votes are being cast for each nominee. As in: "Mr Chairrrrman...The greaaate staaate of Rhode Island...Home of Browwwwwwwwwn UuuuuuuuuuNiversity...proudly casts its votes..."

CHESTER DRAWS

This of course is ironic because studies have shown that 98.3 percent of all Brown students spend their entire four years here not realizing they're in Rhode Island at all, but thinking instead they're in an island off New York.

But as far as national claims-to-fame, we'll always have this:

Our state troopers are the best dressed in America.

One of them even walked the runway - showing it all off - on the David Letterman show.

Take that, humorists of America.

ISN'T RHODE ISLAND IN GENERAL AND PROVIDENCE IN PARTICULAR BIG ENOUGH TO BE KNOWN AROUND THE WORLD?

I used to think that until the time I was in Africa as a journalist. I was trying to hitch a ride on a British RAF flight into the countryside, doing my best to beg for one of few available places by saying I was an important American newspaper writer.

"What paper you work for?" the RAF officer in charge asked.

"The Providence Journal," I said.

I'll never forget his response:

"Is that a religious publication?"

HOW RHODE ISLAND'S NAME CHANGES THE FARTHER YOU TRAVEL

Any Rhode Islander who's traveled has discovered that the more distant you get from home, the longer our name becomes.

Take Providence. In Rhode Island, it's just that: "Providence."

But move into any other New England state, and it gets a little longer: "Providence, R.I."

When you get as far as the Midwest, it becomes, "Providence, R.I., An Hour South of Boston."

Hit California and it's official name expands to, "Providence, Rhode Island, On The East Coast, An Hour South of Boston."

Overseas, in Europe, it's longer still: "Providence, Rhode Island, on the East Coast, near Boston, three hours north of New York, - one of the 13 colonies, in fact, where they used to hold the America's Cup."

However, once you get beyond that, the name gets short again. I've found when asked where I'm from in truly faraway places, like the Middle East or Far East, I don't even try to get into it.

Providence at that point simply becomes, "Near Boston."

WHY DOESN'T THE REST OF THE WORLD NOTICE US?

This problem began on May 4, 1776 when Rhode Island did an astounding thing - it passed a Declaration of Independence a full two months before the rest of the colonies, becoming the first free republic in the new world.

But guess what?

No one noticed.

Then there was the burning of the Gaspee. Long before they tossed a few tea bags into Boston harbor - big deal - some truly bold Rhode Islanders torched an entire British tax ship.

But again, no one noticed.

And they still don't. The Gaspee should clearly bump the Tea Party from textbooks, but historians seem to feel that if it happened in Rhode Island, it couldn't have been that important.

This same kind of thing still happens today, even in mundane areas. like those big, coffee table photo books of New England.

I recently thumbed through a half-dozen at a bookstore and found that while other states got about 40 photos each, we got about five. Often, we get none.

I'd like to know who we see about this.

YOU KNOW YOU'RE A REAL RHODE ISLANDER WHEN...

• Your dream is to move to Florida (Flahrider.)

• You put celery salt on your hot dogs.

• You can pronounce Quonochontaug perfectly.

• But you say "Weyborsett" Street.

• Instead of eating dinner, you start eating suppa.

• You realize that the official name for South County is actually "Way down in South County."

• You put in your will that you want your nickname mentioned in your obituary. (One sharp Rhode Island reader told me she spotted - on the obit page of a single newspaper - the names "Twit," "BoBo," "Smiley," and "Biddy.")

• And if you move north of Providence, you stop going to ocean beaches in the summer and start using local ponds instead. Drive all the way to South County from North Smithfield? F'get abow'it.

• When describing to someone a mutual friend who's been appearing unkempt or unhealthy lately, you say, "He looks like he's been hit by everything but the Fall River bus."

• Your teachers had your parents.

• You know Mayor Cianci personally and prove it by referring to him casually as, "So I was talking to Buddy the other day..."

.• Instead of getting a potato with your entree, you get pasta (pahster) with sauce (source) on the side.

• You've called in to a radio talk show in the last week.

• You're into Keno. And Power Ball. And the drawrin'.

DOES RHODE ISLAND HAVE A REPUTATION
FOR CORRUPTION NATIONALLY?

I think things are better now, but the low point came in the early 90's when a New York businessman named Angela Crawford bought a restaurant in Narragansett.

This was at the height of the credit union crisis and other unsavory publicity like certain mayors of Pawtucket going to prison and Prime Time Live calling us the most corrupt state in the nation.

Anyway, Crawford somewhat secretively applied for a liquor license in his wife's name. When the local liquor board discovered he was the shadow owner, they dragged him in and asked why he was using his wife as a front.

Trying to hide something?

Crawford hemmed and hawed and then came clean. Actually, he explained, the reason is that he was also applying for a liquor license in New York City.

So?

Well, he feared it would tarnish his image if the Manhattan authorities learned he had any Rhode Island connections.

Then he actually added this: "Because of the bad press you've been getting," said Crawford, "I didn't think it would pay to open up a can of worms."

We're talking about the city of John Gotti, but in the eyes of at least one outsider, merely being associated with Rhode Island, even through a legitimate business, would have been the kiss of death.

SOMEONE SAID THE STATE HASN'T GIVEN ITS LEGISLATORS A RAISE
SINCE LINCOLN.

That's hearsay, innuendo and character assassination. They were upped to their renowned $5-a-day during William McKinley's administration.

In 1900.

Some, however, continue to insist that paying our legislators a tenth as much as the janitors who clean up after them is unfair.

To the janitors.

THE ULTIMATE RHODE ISLAND POLITICAL STORY.

Ever wonder how Johnston Mayor (for life) Ralph aRusso got that small "a" in front of his name? It's not a family legacy, it's a political one.

Back in 1964, Ralph Russo (no "a" at the time) decided to run for office and faced a big primary field. Since law dictated candidates be listed alphabetically and pols feared many voters simply pull the first lever, Russo decided to make an extraordinary move.

He had his name legally changed to aRusso.

But this being Rhode Island, where nothing's more serious than local politics, Ralph wasn't the only one willing to go that far. Another candidate named Mario Russillo counter-attacked by legally changing his own name to...this is great...aaRussillo.

Still, Ralph edged him out, kept the name and raised his children with it.

And you can't argue with success - as I write this, he's serving his 10th term as mayor.

THE SECOND ULTIMATE RHODE ISLAND POLITICAL STORY.

In 1983, there was a special dedication in Rhode Island. It took place at La Salle Academy, where many of the state's leaders were shaped.

Everyone was there. First, the sitting governor - Joseph Garrahy. There was the state's Catholic Bishop - Louis Gelineau. Former Cranston Mayor James Taft was there. So was William Dugan, Gov. Garrahy's top assistant. And many others. They all stood together at Smith Street and Academy Avenue - in front of La Salle. And what were they dedicating?

A new wing of the high school?

A local hall of fame?

A noteworthy statue?

No - this is Rhode Island, where it's said many politicians will drive across the state for the opening of an envelope. And frankly, this wasn't too far from that.

What the governor and the bishop and other luminaries were there to dedicate that day was...

A new bus shelter.

And it stands proudly still.

RHODE ISLAND "DISTANCE-PHOBIA" - PART II

• Deborah Watterson of Middletown tells me it's true what they say about Rhode Islanders never leaving their islands - whether it be Block or Aquidneck, which is the island she lives on.

"They speak of the mainland as 'over there,' " she said. "My father-in-law (an islander) packs a lunch before making a trip over any of the bridges. My husband's sister panics at the thought of going 'off-island.' "

Deborah adds that journeying 'on-island' is equally daunting to mainlanders. "I left Peace Dale 25 years ago," she said, "but if I want to see my family (who still live in Peace Dale), I need to go to them. They don't seem to realize that the bridges go both ways. They have occasionally visited me, but they have to drag out the coolers, maps and sleeping bags!"

• When mainlanders do travel to an island, they get in a state of total anxiety, something that Ray Parker, former captain of the Block island ferry, observed frequently. The anxiety, he told me, came out in the form of relentless, almost panicky questions his passengers would ask, as if these "Ocean" staters had never been on a boat before, which was often true.

The most common questions included (He swears he heard these often): "Where does the Block Island boat go?" And: "What time does the 8 o'clock boat leave?" And also: "Does it ever get this rough?"

• But distance-phobia can sometimes be an advantage. A woman we'll only call Donna (Dahner) to protect her guilt, told me of the decision by her Rhode Island inlaws to move

over the Massachusetts line, 45 minutes away. It happened years ago, and ever since, says Donna, in their eyes, the 45 minute drive looms as so daunting that they seldom visit anymore.

Which (this is why I'm protecting her guilt) is fine with her.

"I get much less annoyance from them," she said.

• Sometimes you have to leave Rhode Island to understand Rhode Island. It took moving to Wisconsin for Rich Buonaccorsi to understand about us and distance.

"People here," he wrote me, "find it hard to believe that we (Author's note: Rhode Islanders always refer to themselves not as Rhode Islanders but as "we") don't go to Foxboro to see the Patriots because it's too far. But here (Wisconsin), people will drive four hours or more to see the Packers, and the Packers have been awful for 20 years."

• And a story of my own: My first few years in Rhode Island, I used to drive to Boston routinely for a night out. Then I crossed a mental line and became distance-phobic. I realized it when a group I gave a speech to was kind enough to give me a gift certificate. I opened it up. It was to a restaurant called "The Red Rooster." In North Kingstown.

Instantly, I thought this: "Are these people serious? That's a half hour away." I later wrote a column about it saying I appreciated the gesture, but couldn't conceive of eating there unless I could find a nearby motel room so I wouldn't have to drive all the way from Providence and back the same night. Sure enough, a week later, I got a gift certificate from a North Kingstown motel.

They said they understood.

But you know what? I haven't used either of those certificates yet.

I just can't face the drive.

HOW ABOUT THE MYTH THAT PEOPLE FROM WARWICK RENT BEACH HOMES IN SOUTH COUNTY. JUST A MYTH, RIGHT?

Wrong. Ann Gardiner (all right, she's from Cranston, but it's the same difference) wrote me of a time a friend of her husband Bill visited from North Carolina.

The friend was astonished when he heard Bill mention plans to rent a beach house for a week in Narragansett. In North Carolina, no one thinks twice about driving an hour or even two to go to the beach just for the day.

"You live 30 minutes from the ocean and you are renting a summer home?" he said.

Ann sniffed at that in her letter to me.

"What does he know?" she wrote. "It's at least forty minutes with traffic."

WHAT YOU DON'T WANT TO BE IN RHODE ISLAND

A restaurateur on a rainy night.

NOT OFTEN TALKED ABOUT BUT STILL UNIQUE RHODE ISLAND HABITS

• We hold children's birthday parties at bowling alleys.

• We buy an item at Ann and Hope, find out several days later that it's gone on sale, and proceed to return the original and repurchase another one for the $3 savings.

• When an out-of-stater stops to ask us directions, and we give them a landmark with a funny name, like "Usquepaug," and they ask us how that's spelled, we'll simply repeat the word "Usquepaug" slowly and loudly.

• We abbreviate cities. I can't count how many letters I've received from instaters addressed to me, and then, following my address, "Prov., R.I."

• We drive around in fancy cars with the air conditioning blasting but the sun roof wide open.

• Finally, this one was suggested to me by several people who described themselves as good, devout Catholics but still have a sense of humor about it: Displaying the Blessed Mother on the front lawn in a half-buried bathtub.

THE STRANGE CASE OF THE NONEXISTENT RHODE ISLAND STREET SIGNS

Look close next time you're driving one of the state's main thoroughfares and you'll notice they're not marked by street signs at most intersections. The side-streets along the way are marked, but if you forget the boulevard you'r driving along, you're out of luck. It's just presumed that Rhode Islanders know, so why waste money on signs?

OTHER NONEXISTENT RHODE ISLAND SIGNS.

Lorraine Blomquist told me of driving to a meeting at a small church in the Natick section of Warwick one evening. She couldn't find it though. Finally, she spotted a small white building that looked like a church but had no sign anywhere. So she parked and approached a woman at the door, mentioned the name of the church she was looking for and asked if this building was it.

"It is," the woman said.

So Lorraine asked, "Why is there no sign?"

Without flinching, the woman answered, "We don't need a sign. We know where it is."

I LIKE RHODE ISLAND BECAUSE, PART II

• We were the first state to renounce the crown.

• You don't find this many good restaurants in states twice is big. (Not that many are twice as big; most are 10 times as big, but that's a different discussion.)

• Edgar Allen Poe used to hang out in the Atheneum on Benefit Street.

• And was once told to get lost by a librarian he tried to romance there.

• There used to be a dancing cop at the corner of Dorrance and Westminster who still briefly comes back every so often - usually the holidays - for an encore.

• We have more coastline per person than anywhere else.

• You can have dinner in front of five-foot-tall fireplaces at Newport's White Horse Tavern, the same ones people ate dinner in front of in 1673.

• If you take a four-hour drive in Texas, you're still in Texas, but if you take a four-hour drive here, you're skiing in Vermont.

• You can get Sweet Bread in Fox Point, newly made pasta on Federal Hill, and stroll past past authentic colonial homes on Benefit Street: Where else can you visit three countries - Portugal, Italy and England - within ten minutes? Drive another half hour and you're speaking French in Woonsocket. Or at least being confused by people who speak it, but that's part of our charm.

• People here aren't as impressed with themselves as they are in places like New York and Boston.

• Ted Turner won the America's Cup here in 1977, then drank too much on the way back to dock and had to be carried out of a nationally televised press conference.

• When everyone else leaves Newport in winter, we have it to ourselves. And the same goes for the whole coastline.

THE ULTIMATE RHODE ISLAND STATUS SYMBOL: LICENSE PLATES.

Ask any Rhode Islander what they would be prouder of, driving a Rolls Royce with a nondescript license plate or a '78 Dodge Dart with a low number plate and 90 percent will tell you to keep your lousy Rolls.

Exaggeration?

A few years ago, Paul Pysz, proud owner of a three-digit Rhode Island plate (that's remarkably low by local standards), got the following letter:

"Dear Mr. Pysz," it began. "I am writing in reference to your Rhode Island registration 723. I am a Chevrolet and Honda dealer. Would you be interested in negotiating your registration for a vehicle?"

To protect the guilty, I'll leave out the writer's name. But basically, he was saying: I'll give you a whole car (presumably a brand new one) for your little piece of tin.

Only in Rhode Island.

And what's even more Rhode Island is the postscript.

Paul Pysz, Ocean Stater to his bones, knows what's important in life.

He declined.

DID SOMEONE REALLY ONCE PAY $30,000 FOR A LOW NUMBER PLATE?.

This is the kind of overstated slander that gives Rhode Island a bad name.

It was only $25,000.

For plate number 7.

MY OWN PERSONAL ONLY-IN-RHODE-ISLAND LICENSE PLATE STORY.

A few years ago, I bought a car, and was asked by the salesman what I'd like on my new plate. I told him I didn't want a vanity plate - no personal reference at all, please. Just a generic. I don't know why: something in me just wanted to be low-profile. So I asked for whatever the stick-up men at the ACI were stamping out at the time my plate request came in.

A few days later, the plate arrived. Guess what it was?

MP-228. My initials.

The point is: the poor salesman couldn't help himself. The presumption that all Rhode Islanders prefer vanity plates is so deep that he simply couldn't *not* do it.

I recently got another car, and, still being caught up in an anti-vanity plate mood, asked for a new plate with no personal reference. This time, I made sure there was no misunderstanding.

Please, I repeated: just a generic.

It worked.

REAL RHODE ISLANDER'S CAR

A. ONE LOW BEAM BROKEN, HIGH BEAM MISSING
B. WINDSHIELD PITTED FROM SANDING TRUCKS
C. TWELVE EIGHT-TRACK TAPES (BARRY MANILOW)
D. RIGHT REAR WINDOW INOPERATIVE
E. MOTHER-IN-LAW IN BACK SEAT
F. TRAILER HITCH FOR TOWING QUAHOG SKIFF

DON BOUSQUET

G. BUMPER STICKER: HI NEIGHBOR, HAVE A 'GANSETT!
H. EXHAUST PIPE DRAGGING ON GROUND
I. SNOW TIRES... IN JULY
J. 250+ DOOR DINGS FROM ANN & HOPE PARKING LOT
K. BODY ROT, IN A BIG WAY
L. ONE WHITE WALL TIRE, LEFT FRONT
M. FRONT END SHOT

No vanity plate.

Only I think the Registry punished me for resisting what all good Rhode Islanders are supposed to have on their bumpers.

They sent me the utterly unattractive plate of "UB-600."

Now several people I know have nicknamed me "Ub," the joke being that in Rhode Island, the first two letters of your plate always represents your name, so mine must be Ub.

And many others who don't rib me about it have asked in utter seriousness: "Why do you have UB on your plates? Those aren't your initials."

As a result, I've found myself wanting a vanity plate.

The moral: Rhode Islanders shouldn't fight their nature.

VANITY - WHAT IS THY NAME?

My favorite state vanity plate was given to a Providence urologist named Steven Cohen. You ready? Drum roll please.

"PPMD."

As long as we're on that area of anatomy, there was also a "BRIS-1" out there. I spotted it myself on Route 95. A "bris" is a Jewish circumcision ceremony. But of course, I told myself after noticing the plate up ahead, the car probably belonged to someone named, oh, Brisbane. Or Bristow. Even in Rhode Island, someone who does circumcisions for a living wouldn't advertise it on his car.

But intrigued, I checked on it. And sure enough, it turned out that "BRIS-1" was issued to Yitzchok Dubovick of Providence, rabbi at the time of Congregation Sons of Jacob, a small Orthodox synagogue.

I called him and he told me he was indeed the state's only official "mohel" - pronounced moyl - the Hebrew term for a man who performs ritual circumcisions.

As for why he would put that on a license plate?

He explained it to me succinctly: He's a native.

"I said, 'Why not?'" Dubovick told me. "I'm a Rhode Islander. Rhode Islanders like vanity plates.' "

WHAT ELSE DO RHODE ISLANDERS PUT ON THEIR PLATES?

Someone from Warwick drives around with KOOK - a childhood nickname. Someone else has "DIRTBG." Of course, there's a "QUAHOG" out there. Then there are several so sought after the registry has had to issue over a half dozen of each - as in 1 through 6: two of the more Rhode Island variety are "ACES" and "BABES".

Of course, there's a "WICKED' or two out there.

And as for true vanity, there's an actual "ILUVME." It's owner was asked about this by a reporter once and he insisted the "ME" meant "Maine." Sure.

Several vanity plate owners seem real proud of what nature has done for them. One woman drives around in "MSLEGS," another with "HOTONE." There's also a "BUNS."

And a "BUNS1."

And finally, perhaps the ultimate Rhode Island vanity plate:

"EGOTRIP."

RHODE ISLAND'S MOST TRAUMATIC TIME.

No, not the great credit union collapse. Not the Blizzard of '78. This was far worse. The state was traumatized in 1989 when the legislature pushed the price of vanity plates from $10 to $30, forcing some people to give them up. A Narragansett man named Buzz Vickers who had "BUZZV" for 15 years was among them. A news story at the time quoted him with a comment that captured just how difficult it is for a Rhode Islander to give up a vanity plate.

"It's like losing a relative," he said. "It's terrible. Maybe they should have some kind of a support group for people who had to give up their plates."

FORGET THIS STUFF ABOUT 39 CITIES AND TOWNS; WE'RE REALLY 500 VILLAGES, HAMLETS, NEIGHBORHOODS...

Ask a native who lives on Blackstone Boulevard where he's from and he won't say "Providence" - it's "The East Side."

A native from the Providence College area? No, they're not from Providence either - they're from Mount Pleasant.

And not a single East Providence native lives in East Providence; they live in Rumford (Rumfid) or Riverside (Rivvaside.)

For my first few years in Rhode Island, I thought there was a separate town called Western Cranston, because no one who lives there ever says they're simply from Cranston. That's *Western Cranston* to you, pal.

And a final thought. The advantage of being in a state filled not just with 39 cities and towns but hundreds of hamlets is that if your family lives in Rhode Island long enough, you're bound to get a village named after you.

If you doubt that, just ask the Slocums, the Tuckers (Tuckertown), the Spragues (Spragueville), the Lippitts, the Harrises, the Hopkinses (Hopkins Hollow), the Greenes, the Potters, the Tilllinghasts (Tillinghast Pond), the Perrys..."

THE BASIC UNIT OF MUNICIPAL LAND MEASUREMENT IN RHODE ISLAND

No, it's not city or town. Nor hamlet or village. It's not neighborhood, community, settlement or borough. Nor 'burb.

It's "Parish."

In fact, the parish is more than a unit of land measurement - it's a contained world.

"Out of parish," one Rhode Islander wrote me about her childhood, "was as foreign as 'outtastate'."

YOU KNOW YOU'RE A REAL RHODE ISLANDER WHEN...

• If you're throwing a wedding in Woonsocket and South County guests are invited, you send along a list of local hotels.

• Your favorite adjective is "wickit"

• You've been to several weddings where they served chicken, shells and French fries.

• And even if both bride and groom are Catholic, you consider it a mixed marriage if one is Irish and the other Italian.

• Instead of going on break, you go to cawfee.

• When telling friends something's on sale, you tell them it's on special.

• On Sundays, if you're under 40, you read every wedding announcement in the paper.

• And always recognize at least one name.

• Ditto for the obits if you're over 60.

THAT'S A MYTH, ISN'T IT, ABOUT RHODE ISLANDERS' MOVING ONTO THE SECOND FLOOR OF THEIR PARENTS' THREE-DECKERS WHEN THEY GET MARRIED?

I thought it was a myth myself. Then I got a letter about it from Veronica Platt, a native who sinced moved to Maine.

"As newlyweds," she wrote me, "my husband and I lived on the second floor of my mother's house. My brother Bill and his bride lived on the first floor."

That took up the whole house which made for trouble when her brother Vin got married and needed somewhere to live.

But Vin and his wife found a Rhode Island solution. They spent their first year in *her* parents' home.

It's even said that transplants, envious of the cheap rents, often decide to marry natives because they come with the fringe benefit of this arrangement - kind of a Rhode Island dowry.

SHORTEST CALCULABLE MEASUREMENT OF TIME IN RHODE ISLAND

That between when the light turns green and the guy behind you honks.

DEFINITION OF A CONSCIENTIOUS RHODE ISLAND DRIVER

Those who hit their turning signal two-thirds of the way through their turn.

ARE RHODE ISLANDERS REALLY SUCH BAD DRIVERS, OR DO WE ALL GET THE BLAME FOR THE AGGRESSIVE ROAD HABITS OF A FEW YOUNG MALES?

Ask native Eileen Holland, who moved out-of-state and soon forgot how to drive like a Rhode Islander, which is to say she began driving courteously.

" WELL, SHE'S GOT NEW TIRES, SIXTY-EIGHT THOUSAND ORIGINAL RHODE ISLAND MILES AND THE TURN SIGNAL LEVER HAS NEVER BEEN TOUCHED. "

Then, on a visit back home, she was taking her 82-year-old mother to the mall. They hit a red light where she was due to make a left. When it turned green, Eileen patiently waited like a normal driver for the oncoming traffic to flow by before making her turn.

At that, Eileen's "sainted elderly" (her words) mother laid into her.

"Wuddya doin'?" her mother cried (that's also Eileen's spelling.)

"Waiting for a break in the traffic," Eileen replied.

"Well," she quoted her Rhode Island mother as saying, complete with accent, "y'bedda smottin up and rememba how t'drive around heah. The guy behind us neahly wrecked my new cah. They expect ya t'try to get across. Y'gonna cause accidents drivin' like that."

THE PERILS OF BEING A RHODE ISLANDER OUT OF STATE.

• A friend told me that after her daughter - a native - went away to college, she soon grew terrified at the prospect of people asking her first name. It always went the same way.

She would tell them and they'd look at her confused.

"Cowell?" they'd say.

No, and she'd repeat her actual name.

But they'd say the same thing. "Cowell?"

At last she'd spell it out.

"Oh," they'd say, finally nodding. "Carol. Why didn't you say so?"

• Native Laurie Jones wrote asking me to warn Rhode Islanders against ordering a cabinet or grinder in Maryland. "Unless," Laurie added, "you'd like to be the recipient of some strange looks and, more often than not, some smart remarks: " 'Yeh, honey,' " she was told once, " 'The furniture store's down the street, now you want to give your order?' "

• And there's some advice from Carla White, a Rhode Islander in San Francisco. She grew up using the local word for "cutting" school: "bunking." Recently, she was taking a course at San Francisco's City College when a friend failed to show up.

"The next class," Carla recalled, "I said, 'Ja bunk?' Twenty-plus pair of eyes turned to me. Clearly I was bilingual but in what? Czech? Welch? Uzbek? Only one person in the room could translate, the teacher."

And the reason the teacher knew, Carla said, is that not only was she from Rhode Island, but Cranston itself, epicenter of the dialect.

OTHER PERILS OF A RHODE ISLANDER ABROAD (WHICH IS TO SAY ANYWHERE IN AMERICA BEYOND OUR BORDERS):

• Mention that you're looking for doughboys and people will think you're talking about British World War II infantrymen.

• In Geology class, even if you know the correct answer, you will be seen as an oddball who speaks in tongues when you raise your hand and say, "Cobbin and warta."

• You'll realize it's better to go thirsty than endure the strange looks your new colleagues give you when you ask where the office bubbler (orfuss bubbla) is.

• In Winter, after a snowfall, friends will look at you funny if you say you'd like to head for a hill and go sliding. "Nah," they'll say, "can't. We're going sledding instead."

• At a party, if you suddenly begin to perspire wildly, feel your chest tighten, and tell your host you think you're having a hot attack, he'll likely turn up the air conditioning.

THE PERILS OF BEING AN OUT-OF-STATER IN RHODE ISLAND

• A transplant told me of the moment his very first day in Rhode Island when he sat down at a luncheonette counter and ordered a burger, fries and a Coke.

The waitress set down a bottle of vinegar.

"Excuse me, Ma'm," he said. "I didn't order a salad."

She looked at him. "I know you didn't order a salad."

He tried to remain polite. "Well, Ma'm," he said, "then what's that bottle of vinegar for?"

This time, she glared at him. "Look," she said, "I've had a long day, all right?"

"Honest," he said, "I didn't order a salad."

Finally, recognition dawned on her face. "Oh," she said, "you're not from around here, are you?"

"My first day in Rhode Island," he said.

She laughed. "It's for your fries."

• And Peter Hufstader didn't have an easy time when he set out to take his daughter to a party at a bowling alley soon after moving here. He got lost and stopped to ask directions of a cashier in a Cumberland Farms (Cumblin Fahmz.) She told him the bowling alley was inside a big complex called "Gun City," and directed him there. Just look for the sign, she said; you can't miss it.

He set off, thinking this proved Rhode Island was the capital of organized crime, just like he'd been told. What other place had a gun-oriented shopping area so big it even included a bowling alley so people could relax between purchases of revolvers?

But he couldn't find Gun City. He drove back and forth while his daughter got increasingly upset at missing the party. Finally, he stopped to get his bearings. That's when he looked up and saw a big sign. Suddenly, it dawned on him.

Gun City?

That's exactly what the cashier said.

But he realized his new home state had a unique accent.

And what she meant was "Garden City."

70

STILL MORE PERILS OF BEING AN OUT-OF-STATER IN RHODE ISLAND

• This one comes from Jim Henry, a native now in New York. But he remembers eating at a Rhode Island diner when an out-of-stater stopped in and asked directions to a town called Shep-a-shay.

Everyone told him there was no such place: no Shepashay in Rhode Island.

But the out-of-stater persisted. He knew it existed. At last, they asked him to spell it.

And he did.

Chepachet.

• Sandra Navratil De May, raised in Missouri, personally experienced the perils of being a newcomer in Rhode Island. Soon after arriving, she went into a store and ordered a dark Milky Way.

The cashier looked at her confused. Sandra repeated it again.

"Dark?" said the cashier, still not comprehending.

"A dark Milky Way, please," Sandra repeated. "Dark chocolate."

Then the lights came on in the cashier's eyes.

"Oh," she said. "You mean DOCK chocolate."

• When Janet Phillips - Rhode Islander - was a Brown student, she heard a story from a girl working in the Ivy Room there serving food.

During the crowded dinner hour, while she was at the beverage station, a Midwest student ordered a "Chocolate Bench."

After a moment of silence, with all around staring in confusion, the Rhode Island natives nearby figured out what was going on and began to laugh.

The student had been told the local version of shake was called Cabinet, but the word got mixed up in his mind under the general category of wood furniture, and he mistakenly recalled it as a "bench."

WHY YOU CAN'T EXPORT RHODE ISLAND INSTITUTIONS.

Some Rhode Islanders hold out hope that more local franchises will go national, thereby providing islands of familiarity in the great beyond. But it won't work if - as is unavoidable - out-of-staters staff them.

Picture the Newport Creamery putting an outlet in Boise with Idaho waiters and waitresses. They'll have no idea what Chevul from Creannstin means when she stops in on a business trip for a taste of home and says, "I'd like tawda an orful-orful pleece."

AWARD FOR THE ULTIMATE RHODE ISLAND CONSPIRACY THEORIST.

To Jann O'Leary of Foster who wrote me saying she was convinced Joe Mollicone didn't really spend those 17 months illegally hiding in Utah, but was legitimately held up spending half of it waiting for a table at Twin Oaks and the other half in line at the Registry of Motor Vehicles.

EVEN MORE PERILS OF BEING AN OUT OF STATER IN RHODE ISLAND

• Native West Virginian Paulette Young came here with her Iowa husband for a job transfer. They went to one of the state's landmark restaurants and spotted "quahog" on the menu. Innocently, Paula looked at the waitress and asked, "What kind of pork dish is that?"

• Then there was the time Robert Rogers, a transplant, bought a home in North Kingstown and went to town hall to ask where the electric company was so they could get hooked up.

"A lady behind the desk said to go out Route 102," Rogers recalls, "and turn at the corner where the Wickford rotary *used* to be."

It was bad enough that the directions were based on something no longer there.

But worse, Robert had no idea what a "Wickfit Road-tree" was in the first place.

Of course, he got hopelessly lost.

• Penelope Tuttle Spencer grew up in upstate New York, moved to Rhode Island and took a job as a (what follows is her spelling) "Dispatcha for the Creeanstin Pleece."

She felt she was good at her work but ran into trouble because Roe Dyelandese was her second language.

Once, she dispatched a car to Howard Street; it turned out the call was for Harwood.

Another time she mixed up Knollwood and Norwood since they both came over the phone as Nahwid.

Her worst mistake, she says, was when the Cranston fire department asked for police back-up for a bonfire. Because it was a busy night, she decided that for a routine bonfire, there was no need to tie up manpower. It was a bit hard to explain later why no police were sent to direct traffic around a "barn" fire.

AND YET MORE PERILS OF BEING AN OUT OF STATER IN RHODE ISLAND

• You order a cup of regular coffee, presuming you'll get what the phrase means in the rest of the country: not decaffeinated. Instead, you find the waitress bringing out the Rhode Island version of regular coffee: cream 'n sheuga.

• And a few years ago, there was a widely distributed local ad with a big headline that read: "The Shopper Image," followed by, "The Arcade."

It of course was a play on words, but I got a half dozen letters predicting many Ocean Staters would think the high-end Yuppie store had actually just opened at The Arcade, and that a local ad exec had mistakenly spelled it the way a true Rhode Islander would pronounce it.

WOONSOCKETISMS

• "Side-by-each." (Next to each other.)

• "I live on top of my sister." (She has the apartment below me in the triple-decka.

• "Close the light." (Please turn off the switch.)

• "The next time you cut through my yard, go around." (Enough said.)

• "Bend your head." (Advice to someone walking through a low doorway.)

• "Throw me down the stairs my hammer, you."

• "I'm doing my staws." (I'm going shopping.)

• But there's no truth to the rumor that Woonsocket's Department of Economic Development peddles tourism bumper stickers that say "I Love Woonsocket, Me."

HOW WE REFER TO OUR CITIES, TOWNS, HAMLETS AND 'HOODS

• We never say, "Foster." Or "Glocester." It's always, "Me? I live in 'No-School-Fosta-Glosta.' "

• Few northern Rhode Islanders realize there are such specific places as Charlestown, South Kingstown and Narragansett. It's all South County.

• Make that, "Way down in South County." Or, if you're a Swamp Yankee (Swampa), "Way down Sow' County Way."

• Actually (two-bee onnis witcha), many never even use the phrase "South County" at all. The southern part of the state? It's just "The beach."

• Real Rhode Islanders never say "The East Side." It's "The FASHIONABLE East Side."

• It's never, ever Pawwtucket. It's always, 'P'tucket."

• And always Burraville, Creannstin, Eggs-ta, Chahz-tin, Cumblin, Lih'il Compton, Nawt Smiffeel and Wes-Wawwick.

• Coventry is never Cuvv-in-tree. It's Kah-ven-tree.

• And to most of the state, Portsmouth and Middletown don't exist. All of Aquidneck Island is "Newport." When was the last time someone on the way to Second Beach told you, "I'm going to the beach in Middletown today."

SNOWSTORMS AND BREAD

It's classic Rhode Island lore that at the first sign of snow, we don't buy shovels, scrapers, rock-salt or hats.

We buy bread and milk.

I got to wondering whether this had become more myth than truth, and decided to interview store owners.

It's not myth.

They told me that when the 11 o'clock news confirms a storm is coming the following afternoon or evening, people indeed rush to the supermarket. And not around noontime, either. Many start lining up before opening at 7 a.m.

And sure enough, said the store owners, as soon as the doors open - guess where they head?

I now buy bread and milk myself before storms, though I'm still not sure why. I just know that with snow coming, that's what I'm supposed to do.

Others are equally confused. I once talked to a recent transplant from Vermont. "I don't get it," he said. "When it snows up there, the whole state has a run on ski wax. Down here, they have a run on bread."

The best theory as to why is that the trauma of being caught by the Blizzard of '78, which shut down the state for a week, was so severe it programmed an impulse to buy bread and milk before snowstorms into the Rhode Island genetic code.

Which perhaps explains why a generation that can't even remember 1978 has begun to do it, too.

IS THERE ANYTHING ELSE PECULIAR RHODE ISLANDERS DO DURING STORMS?

• One thing we don't do is leave our property, even if the radio is warning the ocean will come into our living rooms.

"If it did come in," Arthur Clarke of East Greenwich wrote me about Rhode Islanders, "they'd want to be there to shovel it back out."

• A secret known principally to milk store cashiers is that in addition to bread and milk, we also stock up on...chips.

"More the flavored chips," Christine Duffany of the Cumberland Farms on Coventry's Main Street told me. "Like salt-and-vinegar chips, barbecue chips, au gratin chips and, jeez, what do they call them there? Those Doritos."

I also asked a cashier named Irene from Cranston's Oaklawn Avenue Cumberland Farms why chips are big. "Well,'" she said, "they sit and watch TV because there's nothing else to do after a storm. Unless they lose their power; then they're out of luck."

• Finally, there's the ultimate storm trait. If after stocking up on milk, bread and chips, and also batteries, lanterns and flashlights, we then wake up the morning after a storm and find we can easily drive to a well-stocked Dairy Mart, not to mention that our power didn't even go out, deep down, we're disappointed that we didn't need all those supplies after all.

OFFICIAL (AND A BUNCH OF UNOFFICIAL) STATE SYMBOLS

As everyone knows, we have an odd state bird (chicken), an odder state animal (quahog) and oddest of all, a state drink - coffee milk, which left a bad taste in some mouths (sorry) when it barely edged out lemonade slush 49 to 36 in a fierce legislative fight in 1993.

Since the General Assembly is open to such arcane state symbols as a drink, herewith, some nominations for other additions to the list:

Official State Drink With Excess Fat Grams: Awful-Awful.

Official State Hot Drink: Chowda. (Runna-up: Dunkin' Donuts Regular Coffee.)

Official State Mountain: Johnston Central Landfill.

Official State Sangwidge: Grinda.

Official State Treasure: Low number plates.

Official State Concept Still Beyond The Grasp of Most Political Office-Holders: Conflict-of-interest.

Official State Messiah: The Paz.

Official State Income Source: Comp.

Official State Accessory For Men Who Go To Scarborough Beach: Gold neck chains.

Official State Accessory For Cranston High School Girls: Big Hair.

Official State Car Favored By Private School Parents: Volvo station wagon.

Official State Boys' Names On The East Side: Chip.

Official State Boy's Name Everywhere Else: Vinnie.

Official State Road Maneuver: Passing on right.

Official State Source Of Drinking Water: Bubbla.

Official State Source Of Questionable Drinking Water: Pawtucket.

Official State Source Of News About Bizarre (b'zah) Sex: Channel 12.

Official State Home For Ex-Mayors: Leavenworth.

Official State Upper Arm Exercise: Gestures while driving.

Official State Policeman's Breakfast: A chocolate-frosted, a powdered and a cream-filled.

Official State Nightmare Neighbor: Louis Vinagro.

Official State Idea Of Heaven: East coast of Florida (Flahrider).

Official State Source Of Advanced Education: Angelo's School of Cosmetology.

Official State Recreation: Keno, bingo, video gambling, Las Vegas nights, scratch-off tickets, jai alai, the dogs and simulcast racing.

Official State Judicial Dance According To Alan Dershowitz: The Rhode Island Shuffle.

Official State Question Asked By A Co-Worker Before Lunch: Jeet?

Official State Bug: Gigantic blue termite.

Official State Hot Dog: Pawdogs. (Unless you're from the New York System lobby. Of course, if you're from the Saugy lobby...)

HOW SMALL IS RHODE ISLAND? IT'S SO SMALL...

• Five hundred Rhode Islands would fit in Alaska.

• In Texas alone, 64 counties are bigger.

• We're a sixth the size of itty bitty Hawaii.

• Fourteen national parks are bigger.

• Laid end to end, it would take 400 Rhode Islands to stretch the course of America's longest river.

• Our highest hill is only half as tall as America's tallest building.

OUR CONTRADICTIONS.

• Although most Rhode Islanders label state legislators as the most despicable of creatures, everyone's dream of achieving status in life is to become one.

• Although we decry those who get personal favors as a result of knowing someone in government, there are few things we boast about more than getting personal favors as a result of knowing someone in government.

• Although the idea of paying fifteen whole dollars for a parking ticket is an outrage, it's normal to consider paying $25,000 for a tinny, rectangular piece of metal with a single digit on it made by some B&E artist at the ACI.

• Although we are among the most eastern of states, we are filled with names like Wyoming, Nooseneck, Skunk Hill, Bear Swamp, Gull Rock, Bullhead Brook, Snake Den and Locustville.

"LIGHTEN UP... FORTY-FIVE ISN'T OLD. 'OLD' IS WHEN YOU JUST DON'T FIT IN ON SCARBOROUGH BEACH ANYMORE!"

• And although we are the most local, parochial of states, we also have dotted our map with a Lebanon, an Arctic, a Galilee and a Moscow.

• Although in some ways we are an old-world, culturally traditional, patriarchal state, our geography is filled with female names, such as: Point Judith, Betty Pond, Sally Rock, Elizabeth's Spring and Nancy Brown Island. Not to mention Betty Hull Point, May Donovan Marsh, Dollie Cole Brook, Dorothy's Hollow, and, if you'll pardon me, Mary's Seat.

• Although cutting people off in traffic is the favorite state sport, if you manage to catch another motorist's eye, they'll get so instantly polite they'll screech to a halt on 95 to let you in front of them.

• Although our favorite, most inspiring statue is the heroic, noble, "Independent Man," our second favorite is a giant blue termite.

• Although Skahbruh Beach symbolizes a piece of who we are - so does Bailey's Beach.

• And finally, despite our name, we are not an island.

I LIKE RHODE ISLAND BECAUSE, PART III

• We get to eat lobsters any season we want.

• And can even buy them at the dock.

• Claiborne Pell, one of the richest men in the U.S. Senate, rides the bus when at home.

• And always makes sure to use his senior citizen discount pass.

• Despite this blow-dried age, John Chafee, our other U.S. Senator, has never once managed to comb his hair properly. And doesn't seem to care.

• We get to watch RISD kids with purple hair brushing shoulders with East Side matrons.

• Only here can you tune in to a talk show and hear a blue collar woman with a tough, street-survivor accent talking about moving to her summer home, and maybe it's not the Breakers, maybe it's a tiny cottage on the East Providence waterfront, but it's nice to know that not only the super-rich own the coast.

WHY RHODE ISLANDERS CAN NEVER LEAVE RHODE ISLAND BEHIND.

It has happened at least once to everyone who lives in Rhode Island. It happened to me a few years ago in the Caribbean.

I was spending a week on St. Martin, which put me about 3,000 miles from home. In addition, I was at the most secluded hotel on the island. There were a mere dozen guests there. I could not have been more removed.

I finished breakfast and walked to the pool. There were two couples already outside. I sat nearby, began to talk to them and asked where they were from.

"Providence," they said.

You can't leave Rhode Island.

I once brought this up with a sports-writer who just got back from spring training in Florida. One night, he found an out-of-the-way bar and sat down to drink alone. A guy in flowered shorts and black socks sat next to him.

"Hi," the guy said. "I'm from Cranston."

I asked the sports-writer why things like that always happen. He nodded skyward.

"I think it's in the particles," he said.

I got a letter a while back from a Rhode Islander who joined the foreign service. She wanted to truly get away, shake her past, start anew. Her first assignment was Paris. It turned out the ambassador's secretary was from Pawtucket. An isolated coincidence, she thought, and soon she was assigned to a new posting: Geneva. But it happened there, too: the embassy's head of security, a Marine, was from Central Falls.

You can't leave Rhode Island.

WHAT IS RHODE ISLAND - AND WHAT IS NOT

• Ann & Hope is Rhode Island; K-Mart isn't.

• The Pawtucket Circulator is Rhode Island; Route 295 isn't.

FAST BECOMING THE OCEAN STATE'S
TOP TOURIST ATTRACTION !

- May Breakfasts are Rhode Island, power lunches aren't.

- Three-deckers are Rhode Island, but condos are not.

- Quahogs are Rhode Island. Clams aren't.

- Asking for a ballot recount is Rhode Island. Conceding defeat isn't.

- Having a surprise party is Rhode Island. Having a networking party isn't.

- Cabinets and grinders are Rhode Island. Milkshakes and subs aren't.

- Down cella is Rhode Island. The basement isn't.

- A bubbla is Rhode Island, but a water cooler is not.

- Diners are Rhode Island. Bistros aren't.

- Spinach pies are Rhode Island. Spinach salads aren't.

- "Pleece?" is Rhode Island. "What'd you say?" isn't.

- Doughboys are Rhode Island. Cotton candy is not.

- Seeing yourself as a New Englander is Rhode Island. Seeing yourself as an East Coaster isn't.

- Not giving your legislators a pay raise in 100 years is Rhode Island. Giving the governor a mansion is not.

- Coffee milk is Rhode Island. Bosco isn't.

- Calling it "the drawrin' " is Rhode Island. Calling it The Lottery isn't.

- Eating a New York System is Rhode Island. Eating an Oscar Meyer wiener is not.

- Spending $25,000 on a car is not Rhode Island. Spending $25,000 on a license plate is.

RHODE ISLAND MISCONCEPTIONS, TOWN EDITION

• Misconception One: Despite what the immortal Salty Brine said, and what many locals have come to believe, Fawsta-Glawsta is not a single village. It exists only in air wave lore.

• Misconception Two: West Palm Beach, Fla. (West Pom, Flahrider), is not Rhode Island's 40th town.

• Misconception Three: There is no such town as Chariho. This is the name for the combined school districts of Charlestown, Richmond and Hopkinton. There is no truth to the rumor that Glocester, Burrillville and West Greenwich are planning a "deep-woods towns" school district called Globurch.

I LIKE RHODE ISLAND BECAUSE, PART IV

• CCRI's main building looks like the Starship Enterprise.

• In Providence's Cranston Street Armory district, there's a house with huge replicas of crayons mounted on one of the outside walls.

• Mr. Potato Head was born here.

• Not to mention GI Joe.

• Even though Massachusetts thought its idea of "One True Faith" would become the nation's standard, our idea of religious liberty made it into the Constitution instead.

• Newport put up the country's first gas streetlights in 1806.

• "Old" in places like California means 1930, while old here means 1680.

• Ann & Hope is named after the wives of two of the state's first merchants.

• And finally, you can call the governor and can sometimes get through.

• On the first try.

RHODE ISLAND REAL ESTATE

I was once looking through the real estate ads when I came across a home in the "$400's." The ad went on to explain why.

For starters, it was on the Bristol waterfront. It also had its own dock. And then I came across a detail that made me pause. A key selling point in the ad was this:

"Parade Route!"

If you'd just moved to Rhode Island from Montana, that might confuse you. Why would anyone spend over $400,000 on a house that was on a noisy parade route?

Rhode Islanders, however, know exactly what that phrase means. In Boston, affluent buyers are drawn to Beacon Hill brown stones. In Chicago, it's brick Georgians in spacious suburbs. In Rhode Island, it's more basic. If we can watch the Bristol Fourth of July parade from our porch, we'll put our $400,000 on the table.

I called Gerry Carrick, the man from Riker, Farnum & Hill who wrote the ad. He told me that Bristol-based real estate companies use "Parade Route" routinely. Which proves Rhode Island is the kind of place where a wife will actually look at a husband and say: "Vinnie, I know $400,000-plus is high, but it beats fighting the parking problem on July Fourth. Let's buy it."

Meanwhile, the parade route is hardly the only uniquely Rhode Island real estate selling point.

So here are some other potential ads we might just end up seeing one day:

• "Warwick. Storybook cape. Location, location, location! Walking distance to Rocky Point. Mid $500s."

• "Woonsocket: Magnificent five-year-old contemporary. Perfect for would-be Rhode Island attorney. Short drive to Suffolk night law school. $425,000."

• "Developer's dream: convenient to governor's office. A short stroll to ask for special zoning changes or speeding up of environmental review. Mint, 3-bed ranch. $400s."

• "Great eight-room family home, ideal for Rhode Islander worried about stocking up on bread during snowstorm: Next door to Dairy Mart. $300s."

• "Grooming your 10-year-old for the General Assembly? This Mount Pleasant salt box is equidistant from La Salle Academy and Providence College. $220,000."

• "Gracious home, handcrafted cabinets. Ideal for the Rhode Island gourmet who likes to eat big and eat cheap. Next door to annual Pasta Challenge. $290s."

• "The perfect mix: splendor and practicality. Enjoy the ambience of the East Side in your elegant colonial while living close enough to central police station to give regular burglary reports. $495,000."

• "Made-to-order for state and city workers. Save gasoline on all those endless drives to testimonial dinners. Restored Victorian two blocks from 1025 Club. $320s."

• "For the Rhode Island Camaro owner. Impeccable Tudor located between vanity plate application office and Speed Shop featuring discounts on rear- view-mirror Playboy emblems. $244,000."

• "Perfect spot for government officials finishing out time for corruption or ethics violations. Raised ranch 100 yards from ACI work-release office. $175,000."

THE REAL RHODE ISLANDER CHECKLIST, DISTANCE EDITION.

• Although a Rhode Islander for over a decade, you've never been to Block Island (Blah Kyelin.)

• You boast constantly about how ideal it is to live in Rhode Island because it's right between Boston and New York. But you haven't been to Boston in a year and New York in five.

• You hear your married daughter is moving from next door to you in Pawtucket all the way to Warwick and you cry yourself to sleep fearing you'll barely ever see your grandchildren again.

I LIKE RHODE ISLAND BECAUSE, PART V

• John Kennedy married Jackie here.

• The state tax form marks the refund line with a smiling face.

• Gilbert Stuart, who painted George Washington, was born here.

• Our state bird is a red chicken.

• And there's even a monument to it in Little Compton.

• Two monuments, actually.

• And people there have an ongoing rivalry over which one is the official one.

• "Hope" is a much better motto than California's "Eureka," Maine's "I direct" and Connecticut's "He who transplanted still sustains." The only other motto that's almost as good is Colorado's, which is - literally - "Nothing without Providence."

• A 961-pound tuna caught off Matunuck is the largest fish ever brought in by rod and reel in America.

• We passed the first act against the importation of slaves: in 1774.

• We were founded by people who, instead of being sheep, came here because they wanted to run things their own way, which included letting everyone worship the way they darn pleased.

• Captain Kidd once stopped in Jamestown and buried gold there.

• And it's never been found.

• Theodore Francis Green served in the U.S. Senate until he was 93, the oldest ever in either house.

• And Babe Ruth once pitched for the Providence Grays.

"SOME DUDE CALLED ROGER WILLIAMS WANTS TO BUY SOME LAND AND SET UP A SOCIETY BASED ON RELIGIOUS FREEDOM AND DISCOUNT DEPARTMENT STORES."

IT'S NOT REALLY TRUE THAT SOME RHODE ISLANDERS HAVE NEVER TRAVELED TO THE "BIG CITY" OF PROVIDENCE, IS IT?

Well, Jim Byrne was one day driving from his Coventry home when he noticed a neighbor at a bus stop. He asked where she was heading.

"Providence," she said.

He offered her a ride. Then it occurred to him she had a car, so he asked why she wasn't driving.

"She said she hadn't been to Providence in 15 years," Byrne recalled, "and wasn't sure how to get there." This was even though she lived in Coventry - a distance of about 14 miles.

And there was this from Lorraine Chevalier, a native who ventured out into the world beyond Rhode Island, found the distance factor too much and fled back home to Central Falls. "I lived in Revere, Mass. for a very short time," she explained to me, "and hated to go anywhere because everything was more than 5 minutes away."

YOU CAN'T TELL ME THE OLD JOKE IS TRUE: THAT GRANDPARENTS REALLY FEAR LOSING TOUCH WITH GRANDCHILDREN WHO MOVE ACROSS STATE?

No?

Lorraine Bloomquist, URI professor, was speaking with a friend from Wakefield who had decided to sell her home there so she could move near her son and grandchildren.

"They were too far away," the friend explained.

Lorraine presumed they were hundreds or maybe even thousands of miles away.

"Where do they live?" Lorraine asked.

The reply?

"Woonsocket."

True story.

SO WHERE DID THE RHODE ISLAND INFERIORITY COMPLEX COME FROM ANYWAY?

One theory is it's because the way the rest of the country treats us.

Rhode Island will never get over being referred to by the "Wall Street Journal" as a "smudge on the fast lane to Cape Cod."

But the real embarrassing part of that episode was what happened next. A contingent of the state's top officials, including the governor and various mayors, immediately flew to "Wall Street Journal" headquarters in New York to deny we were any such thing. Hard to picture the governor of California would responding that way.

"SIGNS" OF OUR INFERIORITY COMPLEX

Forgive me, but that was a pun. Because as you enter Providence on Route 10 or head onto the new Route 95 ramp in the heart of Capital Center near the old train station, you'll see a curious sign. It tells you what lies ahead in each direction.

North - Boston.

South - New York.

The implication that hits all us local motorists: There's nothing in between.

Do you blame us for feeling inferior?

THE PARADOX OF OUR INFERIORITY COMPLEX.

You'll find few states where natives are prouder of being what they are than Rhode Islanders, and yet...

...and yet there's this paradox...

Many natives, especially around transplants, are apologetic about it.

The other day, I was talking to a woman at a gathering and asked where she was from.

DON BOUSQUET

YOU KNOW YOU'RE A REAL RHODE ISLANDER WHEN...

• When you go to the beach, you spend it not on the beach itself, but in the beach parking lot under an awning by your Winnebago.

• A seltzer man delivers bottles to your home weekly.

• You add a glass-enclosed porch-like parlor to your home and refer to it as "The Flahrider Room."

• In the grocery store, you routinely break egg cartons in half as well as taking one stick of butter, and, grocery cashiers adjust the price without blinking and ring you through.

• You start putting a "The" in front of hospital names. As in "The Miriam," "The Kent," and even, "The Rhode Island."

• You even do it with diseases. As in, "Chollie has the artheritis."

• You refer to pasta sauce as gravy.

"I grew up in Johnston," she said, "and now live in Cranston." She paused a beat, then added sheepishly: "And I admit it."

I've heard that kind of thing 100 times.

There is also this paradox: On the one hand, many natives believe Rhode Island is among the most comfortable, recreation-filled places in America to make a life, but at the same time, they can't quite believe anyone else would actually want to move here.

Jim Byrne Jr. came to Coventry (Kahventree) from Connecticut in 1980. "We were amazed when the natives kept asking us why we moved to Rhode Island," he wrote me. "They couldn't understand why anyone would intentionally come here."

HOW DEEP IS OUR COMPLEX?

I realized how deep the Rhode Island inferiority complex goes when ABC News came to town a few years ago to do a story on our "Biggest Little State In The Union," ad campaign.

I talked to the producer who told me they were initially going to do a wider piece on all the states that were launching promotional ads - complete with jingles. There was "I Love New York," for example, and "Making It In Massachusetts."

But they decided to focus on Rhode Island alone because of a quirk they'd discovered.

All the other state ads, the producer told me, were broadcast exclusively outside the state's border since the goal was to attract companies and tourism.

But Rhode Island's "Biggest Little" ad, he said, was being shown almost solely within our borders.

And so he asked: What's the goal of your Department of Economic Development? Attracting visitors and industry? Or making residents feel better about living where they live.

I wasn't sure how to answer.

ACTUALLY, IT'S NOT AN INFERIORITY COMPLEX, IT'S HUMBLENESS

Recently, a Rhode Island attorney wrote a newspaper commentary saying the state should have had a nationwide search before appointing a new state court administrator.

That, he implied, would have guaranteed the highest quality candidate, instead of just moving up the deputy administrator after the previous guy resigned (due to something having to do with a slush fund.)

Anyway, the new court administrator, Robert Harral, wrote back to the newspaper defending himself. He'd been in court management for 25 years, he said. He was a Ford Foundation Fellow. He'd studied at the institute for court management. He had a doctorate in Public Administration - one of only two court administrators in the country with that. He was adjunct faculty at several state universities. He'd authored articles and had given seminars on court management.

Wow.

You'd think that background would make him one confident person. But then he added this great line that spoke of Rhode Island's...humbleness.

"Although a native of Rhode Island," he wrote, "I hold degrees from schools in New Jersey and Connecticut. A part of my professional career was spent in New York."

There it is: deep down, even the most credentialed natives feel that the ultimate proof of being a major league player is to announce that during their formative years, they actually made it beyond the state's borders.

DO OTHER AMERICANS EVEN KNOW WE EXIST?

Many don't.

Often, we make jokes about people confusing us with Long Island.

I'm afraid they're not really jokes.

Native Celena Illuzzi went off to college at the University of North Carolina in Charlotte. "I often get asked where I am from," she wrote me. "I will say Rhode Island, and 9 times out of ten, the response will be, 'Oh really, what part of New York?' "

THE GREAT ANTI-RHODE ISLAND ROAD ATLAS CONSPIRACY

We're even minimized in official documents.

Take road atlases.

Most states get two big pages. Rhode Island? A fifth of one page. And we never even get our own listing. Flip to "R" for Rhode Island and you'll never find us. You have to figure it out. Hmm. Try Massachusetts. Wrong again.

It turns out we're listed under "C". As in "Connecticut, Massachusetts and Rhode Island." Make sense of that: an "R" state listed under "C."

And I don't even want to discuss how many New England color-photo calenders fail to feature a single shot of Rhode Island.

MORE PROOF OF HOW WE GET NO RESPECT FROM OUTSIDERS

Ira Magaziner, who became chief policy adviser to President Bill Clinton, had earlier run a global consulting firm based in Providence. You could see the reach of his empire on the door of his downtown office.

"Telesis," it said, "Providence, Melbourne, Tokyo and Paris."

But his worldwide staff could never quite accept that their headquarters was in a city like Providence. They would ask him: "Why can't you move to New York, like the other major strategy consulting firms?"

Magaziner's answer: He loved Rhode Island, and this is where he wanted to be. But still his international staff rebelled.

I saw just how much they rebelled when I did a book project with Magaziner and stopped by his Paris office. I glanced at the office door there on my way in, and saw what his French employees had done to cover up the truth about where their company was based.

'Telesis," the sign on the door said, "Paris, Melbourne, Tokyo, and...Boston."

THE ULTIMATE STORY OF HOW NON-RHODE ISLANDERS WILL NEVER GET US STRAIGHT

President Clinton flew to Rhode Island in the Spring of 1994 for a town meeting. He was introduced at the airport by Warwick Mayor Lincoln Chafee.

"Welcome to Warwick," Chafee said.

At that, Clinton stepped forward and, looking at young Chafee, said he wanted to thank the Mayor of Providence. Several people in the crowd corrected him by shouting "Warwick, Warwick."

To which the President reportedly said:

"I'm sorry, I meant to say 'Warren.' "

YOU KNOW YOU'RE A RHODE ISLANDER WHEN...

• Instead of a wiener (weena) with everything on it, you order it "all d'way. "

• When told surprising news, such as that a high state office holder has a love child, you respond, "Geddout." Or, especially if you're female, "No suh."

• You've been to at least one yard sale this month.

• And one Scratch-and-Dent sale this year.

• You take your shoes to the "cobbla."

• You know what a dynamite is. And while in Woonsocket, actually once ate one.

• You consider becoming a lawyer.

• So you begin your application to Suffolk night law school.

• Instead of ordering clams, you order quahogs.

• Not just plain quahogs, but stuffed quahogs.

• Only you don't call them stuffed quahogs, you ask for stuffies.

I LIKE RHODE ISLAND BECAUSE, PART VI

• Bruce Sundlun, multi-term millionaire governor who owns four expensive homes, is still a Rhode Islander at heart and believes a gourmet breakfast consists of two "old-fashion" at Dunkin' Donuts.

• And over the years, routinely has had his limo stop at one on his way to the State House each morning.

• We have a low-key celebrity scene, our biggest stars consisting of guys on TV who tell you whether it's going to rain tomorrow and other guys in airplanes who tell you what route to take to work in the morning.

• Our license plates say we have dibs on the Atlantic Ocean.

• We have the first town in America founded by a woman - Portsmouth - by Anne Hutchinson.

• And Anne, like Roger Williams, was also kicked out of Massachusetts. They accused her, among other things, of behaving more like a "husband than a wife."

DO NON-RHODE ISLANDERS KNOW WHAT A QUAHOG IS?

No.

A local talk show host, broadcasting one day from New York, had a great idea of asking random pedestrians if they knew what a quahog was.

Not one did.

The only one that was even vaguely close said she thought it was a cousin of a crayfish. Most asked whether it was animal, vegetable or mineral.

Then came one earnest intellectual type who said she would use all her college-taught English skills to figure it out and began to brainstorm:

Let's see, she said, quahog. Let's examine this. Hog means someone who's demanding. And Qua? Hmm. That's the prefix to quarters. Voila: A quahog, she triumphantly announced, must be someone on the street who begs for quarters.

YOU KNOW YOU'RE A RHODE ISLANDER WHEN...

• You drive to Dunkin' Donuts to buy coffee, then drive home and drink it next to your coffee maker.

• You don't know the names of your state legislators but could spot John Ghiorse at 50 yards.

• You know a New York System is something you eat.

• In Spring, you put up semi-realistic, life-sized deer statues on your lawn.

• Finally, when asked by out-of-staters why you like living here, you say because it's perfectly located - a short hop to both Boston and New York. But of course, you haven't been to Boston in six months and New York in six years. Too far.

• Even though you're a short hop from some of the country's finest ocean beaches, you have a backyard pool. Raised.

I was once speaking with a Des Moines Register columnist named Chuck Offenburger. We began to exchange local lore. I told him out here, we have an official shellfish - the quahog.

He was silent a moment. "Is that like a pig?"

I told him it wasn't. "It's like a clam."

"Oh. It's not a big seller in Iowa. What'd you call that thing again?"

So no, people do not know what a quahog is.

But I still say they're an appropriate local creature in one respect. Although they live for decades - up to 40 years and more - a Narragansett Bay oceanographer once told me that like true Rhode Islanders, most quahogs end up settling forever within a few yards of where they were born.

WHY DO WE HAVE VICTORY DAY AND NO ONE ELSE DOES?

I have no idea.

But I do know the way you view Victory Day is a means of judging whether you're a real Rhode Islander. When I first moved here, I couldn't believe there was such an unusual holiday - after all, Rhode Island's the only state that has it.

Now I'm the opposite. Each mid-August, I find myself calling out-of-state friends and asking what they're planning for the long weekend.

"What long weekend?" they say.

"It's Victory Day, of course," I say.

Response: "What's Victory Day?"

By the way, it used to be "Victory in ----- Day" but I'm not allowed to say who "-----" is as it was deemed politically incorrect. Which is why we changed the holiday's name to Victory Day.

As a result, every second Monday in August, future generations of Rhode Islanders will end up driving to Lechmere in their Toyotas and Hondas to buy Sony Walkmen, Panasonic Video cameras and Matsushita TVs wondering just who it was we beat.

FUTURE RHODE ISLAND NEWS STORIES WE'RE LIKELY TO SEE

1. "And this just in. Scarborough Beach (Also known as "Skahbruh" and "Johnston-By-The-Sea") was ruled closed today by DEM because of pollution. Tests showed the water contains dangerously high levels of hair mousse, mascara and plating metals washed off neck chains on men. Film at 11.

2. "This is Doug White reporting on Rhode Island's progress as it digs out of last night's snowfall. In one dramatic rescue effort, snowmobiles in Foster are trying to make their way to a snowed-in family who reported being low on skim and Pepperidge Farm Wheat..."

HOW TO RHODE ISLAND

• Make sure you have at least two friends named Vinnie.

• Instead of putting milk in your coffee, put coffee in your milk.

• Eat at Twin Oaks once a week.

• Have a shore dinner at Rocky Point once a year.

• On a hot summer day, instead of stopping the ice cream truck, chase down the frozen lemonade man.

• If someone says something you find surprising, say "Ah you seer-ree-iss?"

• Never refer to Cranston's Park Avenue as "Park Avenue." It's "Pock Av."

• Grumble about how it's time to cut legislators' pay because $5 a day is too much for the bums. If someone tries to steal your business, or your spouse, shrug it off—but if someone tries to take your low-number license plate, hire the best lawyer in the state.

• Never say, "He had a heart attack;" the proper phrase is, "He took a hot attack."

• If you're a teenager, camp out in front of the Civic Center a week in advance so you can be the first to buy tickets to the latest concert.

• If you're over 65, go line dancing.

- If you're the governor, go to every event you're invited to.

- If you're the lieutenant governor, dedicate anything that doesn't move.

- Including bus shelters.

- Unless the governor gets there first.

THE ETHNIC FACTOR

I once spoke with a rabbi's wife who used to live in a mostly Jewish suburb of a bigger city. She was in the majority there. Then she moved to Rhode Island, where the Jewish population is under two percent.

But she told me that here, far from feeling like a self-conscious minority, she's felt more Jewish than ever. I asked how that could be.

She explained that where she used to live, the stress was on assimilation; in Rhode Island, it's on ethnicity, and everyone celebrates that.

The symbol of it for me will always be a downtown place called Murphy's, which for years was a Jewish deli with an Irish name run by a Greek in an Italian town.

JUST WHAT IS THAT THING HANGING FROM THE ARCH AT THE BASE OF ATWELLS AVENUE?

A few years ago, they spent some money fancying up Atwells Avenue and placed a 31-foot-high arch at the foot of it. A large thing hangs from the arch. The thing is six feet long, three feet wide and cast in bronze. Anybody who's ever seen it knows what it looks like - a pineapple.

I wrote that in a column once. The day the column appeared, my phone never stopped ringing.

It's not a pineapple, said a caller, it's a pine cone.

So I printed that in a later column.

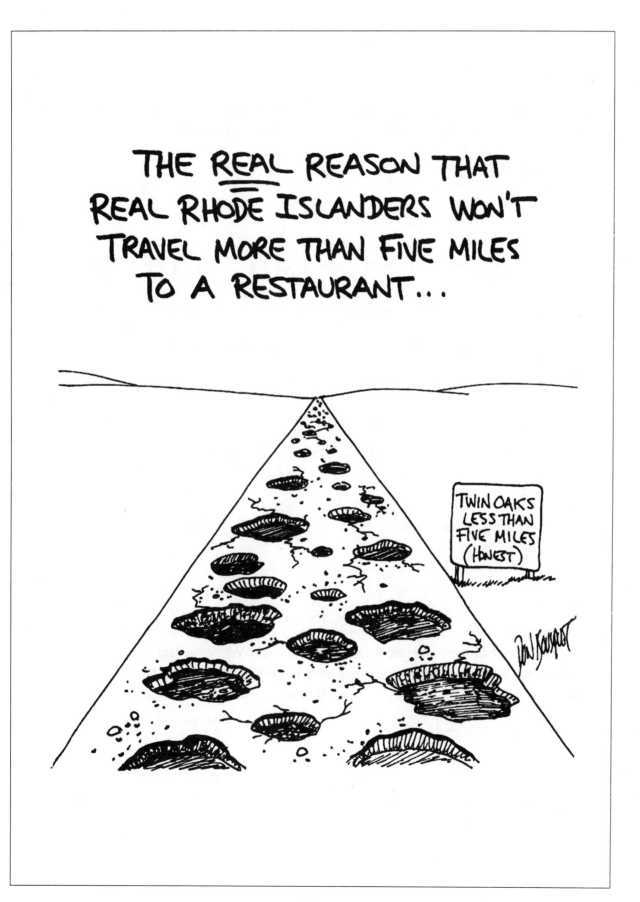

But then others called.

It's not a pine cone, one said, it's a pigna. No, said another, it's an acorn. Several people insisted it's a hand grenade, others a beehive, still others an artichoke.

So to answer the question:

I have no idea what it is.

HISTORIC MOMENTS IN THE ANNALS OF REAL RHODE ISLANDISM:

• June 9, 1772 - British Tax Ship Gaspee burned in Narragansett Bay.

• May 4, 1776 - General Assembly renounces allegiance to Great Britain.

• Oct . 2, 1967 - Midland Mall comes to Warwick.

THE RHODE ISLAND RADIUS

Five miles.

This represents the furthest distance real Roe Dyelindas will travel in any direction from their home to a restaurant.

NEUHSREE RHYME, ROE DYELIN VEUHSION

This was sent in by expatriate Rhode Islander Carla White, in temporary exile in San Francisco. (She's the genius who came up with the phrase: "The Rhode Island Glottal Stop.) Anyway, she said it was her father's favorite nursery rhyme, and it came out this way:

"There was a little geuhl

Who had a little keuhl

Right in the middle of heur fahrrid.

When she was good,

She was very very good,

But when she was bad,

She was hahrrid."

ANOTHER TELLTALE RHODE ISLAND STORY.

I once spoke with a woman who grew up in Manhattan, then moved here with her husband in adulthood. Her entire life, she'd never met a politician - never even got within a block of one. Not a senator, a congressman, not even a city councilman. In New York City, that doesn't happen. It's just too big. Then she arrived in Rhode Island.

Her first month here, she went with her husband to the University Club on Providence's East Side. They wanted to get to the club squash courts, but to do it, they had to go through the men's locker room.

That's routine - you just shout that a woman's coming through to make sure everyone's decent. They did. In the middle of the locker room, they ran right into a man wearing nothing but a towel. Her husband shook the man's hand and made the introduction.

"I'd like you to meet Governor Chafee," he said to his wife.

Three decades in Manhattan and she'd never even seen a zoning board member. One month in Rhode Island, and she was shaking hands with a half-naked governor.

YOU KNOW YOU'RE A RHODE ISLAND DRIVER WHEN...

- You speed up on yellows.

- And pass on the right.

- And yell back at those who yell at you for doing so.

- You turn left from the right lane.

- You're genetically incapable of reading the word "Yield."

RHODE ISLAND SOUVENIRS YOU CAN ACTUALLY FIND FOR SALE

• Lobster claw harmonicas

• Slater Mill back scratchers.

• Rhode Island ashtrays showing a woman reclining by a palm tree with mountains in the background.

And don't get me started about how for my first ten years here, the only local post card I could find was of the Central Providence Post Office.

THE COCKROACH

Aside from the Independent Man, the most prominent Rhode Island statue may well be the huge blue cockroach overlooking Route 95 just south of Providence. It even has a name: "Nibbles Woodaway."

I decided to find out about it and called New England Pest Control, the business that owns it.

They began by telling me it's not a cockroach (or "cockaroach" in Roe Dyelindese), it's a termite.

Then I was given the vital statistics: It's 9 feet high, 58 feet long and 928 times the actual size of a termite.

I asked why they put it up there.

"We think it's gorgeous," I was told.

And how long will it stay.

"We hope forever," the New England Pest Control spokesman said.

And then to show healthy Rhode Island paranoia, he added this:

"It's hurricane-proof."

HOW TO RHODE ISLAND, PART II

- Always eat white clam chowder, never red.

- Own at least one car with dealer plates.

- Obtained through a relative with connections.

- Love the Red Sox, hate the Yankees.

- Always refer to Narragansett Town Beach as "The Pier."

- And Roger Wheeler Beach as "Sand Hill Cove."

- Always get lost on the Pawtucket circulator.

- Ignore parking tickets until you get a court summons.

- Then have them fixed by a relative.

- Who has connections to a Supreme Court judge.

- If you get laid off, quahog.

- Work the second shift sometime in your life.

- Go to at least one testimonial for a politician per year.

- But don't call it a testimonial, it's "A time."

RHODE ISLAND TYPES, PART I: EAST SIDE PREPPIES

Named Muffy, Chip, Missy, Tad, Bitsy, Kip, Buffy, Bif, Kiki or Bink. They go to either Lincoln, Wheeler, Moses Brown, Gordon or PCD. These schools have stringent admission requirements including the need for parents to own at least one Volvo station wagon, and preferably a Range Rover, too.

Boys wear Topsiders, khaki pants, Blue oxford shirt and play Lacrosse.

Girls wear plaid skirts, cable-knit knee-socks and play field hockey.

Half of preppie population summers in Little Compton and beaches at Warren's Point; the other half heads to Narragansett and the Dunes Club.

Mummy plays tennis at the Agawam, dad eats at the grill table at the University Club.

And a Golden Retriever in every house.

RHODE ISLAND TYPES PART II: THE CRANSTON EAST MAN

Often named Vinnie, but one need not be Italo-American to fit this type. Rhode Island high school students call this the "Guido Style."

Usage: "You checked out Tommy? He's totally Gweeded out."

This describes a guy who wears gold neck chains, a black strappy t-shirt and leather jacket. He drives a souped-up Camaro and has a girlfriend named Cheryl (Chevul) with big hair.

Instead of "Hello, how are you today," he says, "Yo."

He begins all other sentences with the expression, "Aaayy."

When he's not with Chevul, he likes to try picking up hot babes at Shooters (Shootas).

RHODE ISLAND TYPES PART III: THE SWAMP YANKEE

Also known as a "Swampa." Unlike the Benefit Street Blue Blood variety of Yankee, Swampas are crusty, frugal, rural, earthy old-style New England types partial to places like South County.

They have names like Zeke and can trace their roots so far back they look upon Roger Williams as an upstart newcomer. They never spend a penny or word more than necessary.

You don't have to be a builder of New England stone walls to be an authentic Swamp Yankee, either - there are plenty who work by day as lawyers and car dealers, then come home, put on their waders, go quahogging and speak in a Rhode Island version of the down-east accent, like the case of the South County Swampa approached by a man carrying a pig.

"Got it for my wife," the man with the pig says.

The Swampa studies on this a few beats, nods straight-faced and allows, "Nawt a bad trade."

One scholar who wrote me about this said Swampas were named for Rhode Island types who hunted in swamps growing up, joined the Colonial army, and specialized in fighting in swamps.

Another letter came in from Carl Manchester Sr. of Jamestown. He told me of asking his grandfather what a Swamp Yankee was.

"A cross between a jackass and a barn door," his grandfather said.

Carl - Swamp Yankee himself - insists it's as good a definition as you'll find.

RHODE ISLAND'S FOUR MAJOR LIQUID FOOD GROUPS

• Coffee milk.

• Del's Frozen Lemonade.

• Quahog Chowder.

• Awful-Awfuls. (Joonya Orful-Orfuls also available.)

FOUR MORE RHODE ISLAND LIQUID FOOD GROUPS

• Coffee Cabinets.

• Iced coffee.

• Dunkin' Donuts coffee - regula.

And finally:

• Coffee syrup (straight up.)

OFFICIAL LOCAL CONDIMENT

• Vinega.

But it only counts on fries.

THREE MAJOR FOOD GROUPS

• Grindas.

• Grindas.

• And grindas.

MORE ABOUT GRINDAS

For those readers who may have just arrived here from Bozeman, Montana, Rhode Island grinders are not something laborers with protective glasses operate at metal shops; you eat them.

At least we eat them here.

They're kind of like a sub.

Or a hoagie.

They're a sandwich eater's sandwich. If you make one with sliced wheat bread, though, it doesn't count. It's got to be on a Torpedo roll the size of a large Dachshund. And it's got to have enough heavy ingredients to necessitate a triple bypass afterward, or at least an angioplasty.

Meatball grinders are among the favorites. But it's not enough to have meatballs alone. You've got to cover them with spicy sauce. Preferably red.

If you're a serious grinder eater, you get the works, which includes, meatballs, Italian salami, hot peppers, hot relish, pickles, oil, onions, tomatoes, lettuce, provolone, oregano, pepperoni, prosciutto and something called capocolla, which is Italian ham.

And maybe top it off with some vinegar for a little flavoring.

Oh - did I mention celery salt? Never forget the celery salt.

THE RHODE ISLAND SANGWIDGE

See "Grindas" above.

Though if you call it a sandwich, you're allowed to use wheat bread.

You're not, however, allowed to call it a Roe Dyelin sangwidge if you simply fill it with turkey and mayo.

You have to go ethnic.

In most places, order an eggplant parmesan sandwich on white, and you might cause a riot.

Here, no one would blink.

YOU KNOW YOU'RE A RHODE ISLAND DRIVER WHEN...

• You haven't gone under 70 on an interstate since 1979.

• Except for those times you were daydreaming at 45 miles per hour.

• In the high speed lane.

• And you weren't even polite enough to notice everyone scowling at you as they passed you on your right.

• At stoplights, you charge left in front of oncoming traffic the instant you get a green.

• At stop signs, you do The Rhode Island slide.

• And you're an expert at The Rhode Island Block: When attempting a left turn from a parking lot into heavy traffic, you pull out as soon as there's a break on your left, then just sit there for three or four minutes blocking cars while you wait for the traffic coming from your right to clear.

THE DYNAMITE

Rhode Island may be the smallest state, but when it comes to food, it's splintered into countless ethnic enclaves. The Dynamite, for example, is the Woonsocket variation of the grinder.

The Dynamite is known for having a bit more kick than your average grinder, or jar of battery acid, so you might want to toss in a little chili powder to make it official.

And go heavy on the sauce.

Instead of grinder-style meatbowls on your Dynamite, hamburg is often preferred.

That wasn't a typo, by the way. Rhode Islanders don't refer to hamburgers as "hamburgers." We call them "hamburgs."

Or more accurately, "hambeugs."

THE PERILS OF TRYING TO GET A RHODE ISLAND SANGWIDGE WITHOUT EVERYTHING ON IT.

Linda Haverty of Middletown told me of the time she was a regular for lunch at a local D'Angelo's sandwich shop.

She started ordering a #9 Pocket - steak, cheese, peppers and onions. Only she asked for no onions. The counterman nodded and made the sandwich, only when she began eating, she discovered there were onions inside.

Next time, she was explicit: No onions.

But again, onions. This went on for weeks, and every time, the same thing happened.

She ultimately decided it was part of Rhode Island culture: people who make steak-and-pepper sandwiches in this state are not capable of *not* adding onions.

"It was just so Rhode Island," she said.

She added that she found there was only one solution.

She began ordering a different kind of sandwich.

THE SHAW DINNA

Some here say the closest thing to a secular temple in Rhode Island is the Rocky Point Shore Dinner Hall, consecrated to the worship of clamcakes and chowder. And corn and fries. And cole slaw. And baked fish with creole sauce. And don't forget the boiled lobster, boiled chicken and linguine with clam sauce. And fish and chips. And did I mention the Indian pudding and watermelon?

After the above is consumed during early evening services, it's traditional to ride the Plunge and the Corkscrew roller coaster.

Then you eat a doughboy - a ring of fried fat the size of an El Dorado hubcap - and call it a Rhode Island night.

RHODE ISLAND'S VERSION OF FAST FOOD: FAST FISH

The standout example is clam cakes. They were made famous by the Rocky Point Palladium which has a special window offering an elaborately well-thought-out menu of Rhode Island choices giving you the option of clamcakes, clamcakes, clamcakes or clamcakes.

DECIDING WHAT TO ORDER FOR DINNER, RHODE ISLAND VERSION

"Stot with chowda, Chollie?"

"Fine, Dahris, and maybe we split a plate of stuffies. You want anything else for an app?"

"Maybe some steemiz and clamcakes. But only if they have the lih'il necks. What do you like for the main cawse?"

"Not a grinda, I had one for lunch: sorsage and peppiz."

"Let's go with a New Yawk System, Chollie. Or do they seuhve Saugies here?"

"What difference? Wenniz ah weeniz. They're all bellybustiz to me."

"Weeniz ahnt weeniz, Chollie. There's nuthin' like a Pawdog."

PHIL'OL MAN' HENDRICKS OF BRISTOL PASSED ON AFTER BEING THE FIRST HUMAN TO MAINTAIN A STRICT RHODE ISLAND DIET ALL HIS LIFE — CONSISTING OF ONLY JONNY CAKES, DOUGHBOYS, CABINETS AND CLAM CAKES...

...PHIL WAS FORTY-ONE.

DON BOUSQUET

YOU KNOW YOU'RE A RHODE ISLAND DRIVER WHEN...

• And you generally regard most traffic signs merely as suggestions.

• You take two spaces in a parking lot to keep your paint job from getting a ding.

• Even though the directions tell you to put your registration stickers in the lower right corner of the plate, you plaster them in every conceivable piece of white space - including the centers of the O's and zeroes.

• You have a bumper sticker that says, "Rhode Island State troopers, Always There When You Need Them," not because you're a great State Police booster but because you think it'll avoid tickets.'

• On interstate entrance ramps, you come to a full stop before heading onto the highway.

"But Pawdogs ahnt gaggiz. Too small. You want gaggiz, you have to go to Haven Brothers."

"I'm sure the weeniz here are fine."

"As long as they come with hot, spicy thick meat sauce, some chopped onions and plenny of cehrry sawt. A hot dog in Roe Dyelin's not a hot dog if all you do is put mustit or ketchup on it."

"What do you want for a vegetable on the side?"

"Can't decide between a t'mayta pie or a spinach pie."

"Why don't we both just get snail salita?

"Maybe baked ba'day'diz with sowwa cream?"

"Akchili, I'm in the mood for pahster with red g'vavy."

"Sounds great."

"And deseuht?"

"Zepolle?"

"Zepolle it is."

"Sounds like a lot to eat Dahris."

"Don't eat too much, Chollie. I'm planning a big Rhode Island breh'fiss t'marra. Got in a new batch of Jonnycake mix from Uncle Richit in Usquepaug."

TRULY ULTIMATE SIGNS THAT YOU'RE A REAL RHODE ISLANDER

• You rent a stretch limo - white - to drive you two miles from your home to see Sinatra at the Civic Center.

• You know how to probe for quahogs with your toes while walking the shore.

• You've not only been to a "Time" (testimonial) at the 1025 or the Venus - you've even had a Time thrown for you.

126

"STOP COMPLAINING. YOU KNEW I WAS A
RHODE ISLANDER WHEN YOU MARRIED ME!"

- Though you have no connection with the sale of automobiles, you get a dealer plate.

- You've cruised with Arlene.

- And Salty.

- And the Bishop.

THE RHODE ISLAND QUIZ

Answers on next page. (A handful of these will be easy if you've read closely up until now.)

1. Name a former Rhode Island congressman and a current mayor who wear toupees.

2. What's the highest hill in Rhode Island? Within 150 feet, how high is it?

3. What's the Rhode Island state flower? (Hint: Think talk show hosts.)

4. Which sailboat lost us the America's Cup?

5. What do you call the scoop a quahogger uses to get quahogs?

6. Within 50 years, name the year Rhode Island was settled.

7. What's the license plate number of Buddy Cianci's mayoral car?

8. The Pawtucket Red Sox won the longest game in the history of organized baseball. How many innings?

9. Name the most common career choice among Central High female graduates, as chronicled in past surveys.

10. What's Rhode Island's most popular beach?

11. What town has the official monument to the Rhode Island Red?

12. Which Newport mansion was used in the filming of both "The Great Gatsby," and, "The Betsy?"

13. What was the The Gaspee?

"OH, LOOK, HOWARD, STEAMED CLAMS!
MY HOWARD HAS AN ALMOST UNNATURAL
FONDNESS FOR STEAMERS..."

14. Where was Rhode Island's first State House, and what is it now called?

15. What epitaph is inscribed on horror writer H.P. Lovecraft's tombstone in Swan Point Cemetery?

16. Within five inches, what's the official measurement taken at Green Airport of snow that fell on Rhode Island during the Blizzard of '78?

17. What was the name of organized crime boss Raymond Patriarca's Atwells Avenue business?

18. Name six of the 14 islands in Narragansett Bay.

19. What is the only National Park in Rhode Island?

20. What is this state's official name?

21. Name all eight cities in Rhode Island.

22. What are jonnycakes made of?

23. Within five miles of each, guess the greatest length of the state and the greatest width.

24. What piece of clothing is the Independent Man wearing?

25. And what objects is he holding onto?

ANSWERS TO THE RHODE ISLAND QUIZ

1. Eddie Beard and Buddy Cianci.

2. Jerimoth Hill, in Foster, 812 feet.

3. Violet.

4. Liberty.

5. A bullrake.

6. 1636.

7. 10000

8. 33.

9. Cosmetologist.

10. Scarborough Beach.

11. Little Compton.

12. Rosecliff.

13. It was a British tax ship.

14. In Newport. The Old Colony House.

15. "I am Providence."

16. 27.6 inches.

17. National Cigarette Service, Coin-O-Matic Distributing Co. or National Vending Co.

18. Aquidneck, Prudence, Patience, Rose, Hog, Conanicut, Despair, Dyer, Goat, Gooseberry, Gould, Hen, Hope, Dutch.

19. The 4 1/2 -acre Roger Williams Memorial on North Main Street in Providence.

20. The State of Rhode Island and Providence Plantations.

21. Providence, Pawtucket, Cranston, Warwick, Woonsocket, East Providence, Newport and Central Falls.

22. Cornmeal.

23. Length - 48 miles. Width - 37 miles.

24. A loin cloth or a rumpled skirt.

25. A spear in one hand, an anchor in the other.

THE "ROE DYELIN" QUIZ

1. What's the traditional evening meal called in Rhode Island?

2. Young male Roe Dyelinda's vehicle of choice?

3. Young male Roe Dyelinda's greeting of choice?

4. Young male Roe Dyelinda's expression of choice?

5. Second favorite?

6. Roe Dyelin version of "pardon me"?

7. Young female Roe Dyelinda's version of "no"?

8: Some say that symbolically, Roe Dyelin actually has 40 cities and towns, not 39. The 40th? (Hint: "West Pom" is its epicenter.)

9. What has the power to make every quart of milk in Rhode Island disappear within an hour?

10. And now an easy one. You're in a public building and you're thirsty. What do you ask for?

ANSIZZ TO THE ROE DYELIN QUIZ

1. Suppa.

2. Shuvalay Camavvo.

3. Yo.

4. Aayy.

5. Oo-dee.

6. Pleece?

7. No suh.

8. East coast of Flahrider.

9. Snow flurries.

10. Bubbla.

WHY YOU CAN NEVER LEAVE RHODE ISLAND IN SPIRIT EVEN IF YOU LEAVE PHYSICALLY.

A strange phenomenon began to unfold for Don Bousquet and I when we went to bookstores to sign the prequel (I've always wanted to use that word) to this book. I'd say a full third of those buying were sending them to ex-Rhode Islanders around the country.

Why?

The buyers explained that no matter how far these friends and relatives had moved, and how long they'd lived there, deep down, they still considered themselves Rhode Islanders, and ached for stories of local lore.

And here's the real kicker. Of the letters I got from people who read "The Rhode Island Dictionary" and wanted to suggest other native quirks and traits, a good one-third were from out-of-state. And almost all said the same thing: even after 20 years in the upper peninsula of Michigan, or down in Mobile, Alabama, or way out in Seattle - they missed "home."

That's their word.

Home.

Many correspondents who felt this way weren't even natives; they'd spent the first part of their lives in say, Philadelphia, and the last 10 years or so in Dallas. But they didn't see either of those places as their identity. It was that 10 years in the middle they spent in Rhode Island that got hold of them and will forever make them feel this is the state they're part of.

"I grew up in New Jersey and now live in California," one reader said. "But I'll always be a Rhode Islander."

As will all of us who have lived in this state, and loved this state - wherever we may end up.

DON'T
KID YOURSELF, YOU'RE
LEAVING
RHODE ISLAND
AND YOU JUST
MIGHT LIVE
TO REGRET IT.!
DON BOUSQUET